"The guidance in this boc
on how to get from *A* tc
have been instilled with
journey until Jesus calls us home to be with Him. God
has taken Edwin on a pilgrimage that has sealed his
passion to help others see the ambush the enemy sets in
front of all who blindly walk into his traps. May all who
read these pages be encouraged and blessed as I was and
will continue to be."

—Bob Morales
Associate Pastor, Light of the World Church,
Shawnee on Delaware, Pennsylvania

"The subject of walls is a delicate topic in our world
today. We have all dealt with walls in one form or
another. Whether your walls have been spiritual or physical, Edwin's work, *Restoring the Walls*, is sure to challenge
you to grow. I believe without a doubt that you will grow
spiritually after you read this book. This work is destined
to begin a revolution in you!"

—Efrain Figueroa
Executive Director of New Life of New York City

"In both our society and personal lives, walls can serve the purpose of building us up in God's intended purpose or dividing us from it. In this book, Edwin unpacks that idea beautifully. Using the thought-provoking and inspiring story of Nehemiah and his band of misfits who 'had a mind to work,' Edwin gives much-needed and well-executed advice for the body of Christ today."

—Todd Korpi
Urban Missiologist,
Author of *The Life-Giving Spirit: The Victory of Christ in Missional Perspective*

RESTORING
THE
WALLS

How to Rebuild and Renew Your Relationship with God

Edwin J. Perez
Foreword by John Blondo

LUCIDBOOKS

Restoring the Walls
How to Rebuild and Renew Your Relationship with God

Copyright © 2018 by Edwin J. Perez

Published by Lucid Books in Houston, TX
www.LucidBooksPublishing.com

ISBN-10: 1-63296-217-9
ISBN-13: 978-1-63296-217-1
eISBN-10: 1-63296-223-3
eISBN-13: 978-1-63296-223-2

Special Sales: Most Lucid Books titles are available in special quantity discounts. Custom imprinting or excerpting can also be done to fit special needs. Contact Lucid Books at Info@LucidBooksPublishing.com.

Dedicated to my beautiful wife, Jocelyn,
and my two boys,
Elijah and Ethan.
May the walls of our love forever surround us.

Table of Contents

Foreword

Jesus pursues those forgotten by everyone else. He lifts the bruised and brokenhearted. He speaks life and beauty into their reality.

To encounter Jesus is to begin to see beyond the natural—to know with certainty that I am already seated in heavenly places with Christ. True living begins with a posture of rest knowing that I am blessed with every spiritual blessing in Him.

Some see impossibilities. Others live miraculous lives defying every word of doubt spoken against them. Edwin writes from a place of close encounter with God and with a clarity that invites others into the reality of union with God's Son.

Deep relationship with God begins with understanding that He has chosen us and desires that we experience Him in His fullness.

David got God's attention as he worshiped out in the open wilderness caring for his father's sheep. He was anointed to lead a nation and set apart to reveal the heart of God to his generation. Opposition. Adversity. Running for years as a fugitive from a leader determined to destroy his destiny in God. All of this marked David in his journey to the palace.

Rejection causes many to build walls. Undeserved anger and criticism sting. David openly exposed the brutal pain of being betrayed by one closest to him. Yet in all this, God was forming David's inner being and working every detail for its supernaturally intended purpose.

God intends to build and form you into the substance of His son. Your perspective is transformed as you realize that the people placed in front of you are positioned by your perfect loving Father in heaven who has declared His design to release ever-increasing favor over your life! This awareness births freedom within us. Nothing is just happening to me. The walls in front of me and those I have constructed within me are not greater than God's purposes for me.

Christ frees you. Free from sin. Free from accusation. Free from bondage to the approval of people. Free to live with overflowing joy. Free to give yourself to God and others with authenticity. The real you. All in.

David keeps it real. The songs he wrote are cherished because they are raw. They express passionate devotion and adoration. They also scream in pain, cry in loss, question with doubt, and acknowledge the surrounding darkness.

Not only does God not run from David's pure conversations, He comes close. He sits near. He speaks gently.

God speaks to us most clearly and beautifully through Jesus Himself. Jesus was willing to empty Himself and humble Himself to the point of taking the curse of our sin upon Himself on the cross. To call us as His bride into intimate union, He laid His life down.

In doing so, He destroyed walls of hostility. The veil in the house of God was ripped in two. Men and women who were separated by religion and ethnicity are now able to be one with God and to live in unity with each other.

This is the invitation of this book. As you enter the journey of what God has downloaded into the heart of Edwin, you will see Jesus active in the life of a man committed to Him. He will take you to the Great Wall of China and the newly restored walls of Jerusalem. He will probe deep into how you think by asking specific questions. Embrace the journey of where God wants to take you today.

As you encounter the author experiencing loss at 16 years old, walking in obedience to restore relationships, raising his boys, and sitting with Jesus, you will hear the loving voice of Jesus speaking to you. You don't need to remain brokenhearted. You were chosen to experience the beauty of the Son. Give your attention to Him. Give Him your yes. Prepare to experience His glory!

John Blondo
Lead Pastor at Bethlehem Church,
Queens, NY

Introduction

Walls are part of our lives, whether they are physical or spiritual in nature. They can separate us or serve as necessary boundaries, helping us grow stronger together. This book was written to show how we depend on walls and sometimes must even rebuild our own walls to better fit God's design for our lives.

The first part of this book will help us see how walls function on our spiritual journey, sometimes serving a good purpose but other times causing unnecessary divisions. We'll consider the role of walls in the book of Nehemiah and how walls relate to restoring the broken pieces of our lives and rebuilding our relationship with God through the practice of spiritual disciplines.

The second part of the book will look at walls by examining a couple more stories from the Old Testament. First, we'll consider Daniel's encounter with Belshazzar and the writing on the wall, applying its lessons to today. Then, we'll explore the walls of Jericho coming down and Joshua's charge to possess the Promised Land. The remaining chapters will bring everything together by focusing on how we can love and serve Jesus with all our heart, soul, strength, and mind.

Dear reader, it's with great gratitude and a humble heart that I write this book, hoping to help us grow in the grace and knowledge of God. I believe concealed spiritual walls can hinder our progress and leave us feeling isolated and disconnected. But purposeful, godly walls can help us walk more closely with the Lord, bringing him glory.

Chapter 1

The Walls That Divide Us

"All these were cities fortified with high walls, gates, and bars, besides very many unwalled villages."

—Deut. 3:5

In the third century BC, one of the most recognized symbols of China, and indeed the whole world, was constructed—the Great Wall of China. One of the "New7Wonders of the World," the wall spans some 4,000 miles and is 15–30 feet high in most places. It is the world's largest man-made structure. China's Emperor Qin She Huang ordered the building of the wall to keep out barbarian invaders. Little did he know that the wall would not actually prevent invaders from entering China. It served more as a psychological barrier between

China and her enemies than an impenetrable line of defense. It was designed to preserve the Chinese culture from Western civilization and separate the people from any kind of outside influence. Despite the great lengths they took to prevent their enemies from coming in, the wall came up short and couldn't do the job.

It's common to put up walls in nearly every facet of life. Whether physical, emotional, or spiritual, walls are part of our lives. We want to feel secure and in control, keeping a safe distance from the intrusions of others, sometimes even friends and family. Why do we go to such great lengths to avoid people if Christ calls us to love others? In our effort to stay in our comfort zone, have we ignored Jesus's call to be salt and light in this world?

Don't Get Too Close

Living in New York City, I have frequently taken the subway in order to avoid the brutal traffic. After making my way into the dark cavernous MTA (Metropolitan Transportation Authority) system, walking along the steel corridors and going down the slippery steps, I have sometimes been confronted with such a horrible smell that I could hardly stand it. To my dismay, it has been a person near me, dressed in old, worn-out clothing and passing from train to train to gather a few cents to buy something to eat. My first reaction was not what you would call Christlike. In fact, it was the total opposite—my flesh just wanted to distance myself from someone society considers an outcast. The closer I got to him, the stronger the smell. It was plain to see that everyone else was trying not to get too close.

The way we treat others and our approach to life need to be examined in light of scripture. If someone or something doesn't fit into our agenda or the norms of our community, we tend to automatically erect a wall, forbidding further entry. Thinking in such a closed-minded way can result in pride and self-righteousness, and those attitudes smell odious to God.

The centrality of the image of God is crucial to how we think about ourselves and others. Every person you see is made in the image of God and therefore has great dignity and worth. We are meant to image God in the world as well as in our relationships, which means being a source of love rather than judgment and division.

> The centrality of the image
> of God is crucial to how we think
> about ourselves and others.

Admittedly, getting close to others can put us in a more vulnerable position. There is a cost to choosing engagement and love instead of selfishness and isolation. But that is God's agenda for his people. After all, Jesus came all the way from heaven for us. Along the same line, Paul wrote, "But now in Christ Jesus you who once were far off have been brought near by the blood of Christ" (Eph. 2:13). Paul was speaking to Gentiles who were alienated from the community of God and without hope. In Christ, these outsiders were welcomed into the new community comprised of people from every nation, tribe, and tongue. The walls of division between Jews and Gentiles had been broken down.

Divide and Conquer

The great Baptist preacher Charles Spurgeon said that division is often the work of the enemy. "Satan always hates Christian fellowship; it is his policy to keep Christians apart. Anything which can divide saints from one another he delights in. He attaches far more importance to godly fellowship than we do. Since union is strength, he does his best to promote separation."[1] The enemy tries to cause division and disrupt unity. He knows his time is limited (Rev. 20:10), so he will try anything he can to prevent the church from succeeding in its mission.

The church in Corinth was dealing with dissension and growing factions, so Paul addressed them forcefully: "I appeal to you, brothers, by the name of our Lord Jesus Christ, that all of you agree, and that there be no divisions among you, but that you be united in the same mind and the same judgment" (1 Cor.1:10). Unfortunately, the echoes of division in the early church can still be heard in the church today. Conflict within ministry continues to occur in every shape and form. Too often, small decisions get blown out of proportion.

The common goal for every Christian should be God's glory and not our own. Our focus should be shifted to exemplifying Christ in our character and lifestyle. We tend to forget that and instead argue and divide over things that don't really matter. The notion of Christ being divided goes against his very nature, and it's certainly not what he intends for his people. In the Gospels, Jesus said that he was one with the Father. We see all three persons of the Trinity unified as one and working together at Jesus's baptism.

We also see the importance of unity in the relationship Jesus had with his 12 disciples. He chose 12 common working men to follow him. He ate with them, walked with them, and empowered them for ministry. They were constantly with him (other than when he managed to slip away to pray, and then they went looking for him). The close bond Jesus shared with his disciples would transform them into men on a mission to share their lives with others and expand God's kingdom. God would use this rag-tag group of disciples to launch a missionary movement that would change much of the known world. And it all started with these men spending time with Jesus, learning from him.

In light of how crucial unity is to the church, you can see why the enemy tries to bring division. He tries to divide and conquer the church, encouraging dissent among Christians. It's a tactic used in military operations to try to separate and weaken the enemy. And yet God is stronger than the enemy, and even when things look bleak, he is able to secure the victory for his people.

The song of Moses in Exodus 15 is a beautiful rendition of how God shattered the walls of 400 years of oppression, conquering the enemy for his glory and the freedom of his people. Exodus 15:9 reads, "The enemy said, 'I will pursue, I will overtake, I will divide the spoil, my desire shall have its fill of them. I will draw my sword; my hand shall destroy them.'" But that's not how things went down. Instead, Moses and the people of Israel were left singing, "I will sing to the Lord, for he has triumphed gloriously; the horse and his rider he has thrown into the sea" (Exod. 15:1).

So while the enemy attempts to cause division and strife among God's people—and appears to be succeeding at times— he will not ultimately succeed because the battle belongs to the Lord (2 Chron. 20:15), death has been swallowed up in victory (1 Cor. 15:54), and the walls of division must come crumbling down at the feet of Christ.

Doctrines That Divide

In his book *The Doctrines That Divide*, Erwin Lutzer tells a story that illustrates how a single letter or comma can change the meaning of a message. Back in the days when messages were sent by telegraph, there was a code for each punctuation mark. A woman touring in Europe cabled her husband to ask whether she could buy a beautiful bracelet for $75,000. The husband relayed the message back "No, price too high." The cable operator, in transmitting the message, missed the signal for the comma. The woman received the message that read, "No price too high." She bought the bracelet; the husband sued the company and won. After that, users of Morse code spelled out punctuation.[2] A comma or an iota can make a big difference when communicating a message.

Communicating the gospel message has become more complicated since the early church days due to doctrinal debates and cultural baggage surrounding people's understanding of Christianity. So how can we share the good news with clarity and conviction, focusing on what truly matters most? When we read the New Testament, we notice that Jesus spoke with unusual authority, unlike the other religious leaders. And frequently, he spoke in parables—earthly stories with a spiritual point. These stories captured people's attention while challenging them to consider profound spiritual truths. Of course, not everyone understood or appreciated his parables. In fact, even his own disciples questioned this approach because of their own spiritual dullness (Matt. 13:13–15). Nevertheless, we see that Jesus communicated his message of hope and love with simplicity for all to hear. Unfortunately, we tend to complicate the simple gospel message with doctrinal debates and legalistic rules that turn people off from our message.

If Jesus is not the center point of our message, then we have failed in our delivery, and our words will fall on deaf ears. I'm not saying that we shouldn't say hard things. Sometimes preachers are tempted to skip certain passages of scripture that speak of God's judgment in order to have a more seeker-friendly church. Jesus certainly preached the good news of the gospel, but he also spoke of hell more often than heaven. So we must not shy away from speaking hard truths. It's the unnecessary debates and controversies that we need to avoid.

It's a matter of knowing your audience and knowing what God is calling you to say to them. Doctrinal debates have their place among Christians, but trying to explain every doctrinal nuance to new believers or people who haven't yet come to faith shouldn't be the main crux of your message.

A strong foundation of discipleship—what it means to follow Jesus—should be fostered rather than getting bogged down arguing about predestination, free will, or the proper subjects of baptism. Why talk about these controversies when so many people don't understand the basics of the faith?

Christianity is a religion that is founded on the good news that hope can be found, life can begin anew, and love is everlasting. Doctrine refers to the theological truths the Bible teaches and Christians believe. (1 Tim. 1:10; 4:16; 6:3; Titus 1:9). Sound doctrine is vital to our faith, but it is also meant to shape how we live and treat others. People are not going to listen to a person who's confused about what he or she believes and isn't able to present a clear message. Nor will they want to become a part of a group like a church if it has a muddled message.

> Let's not commit the sin of craving controversy but rather have conviction about what we believe, preferring quiet confidence to quarrels and firm faith to friction.

And then there's the more serious issue of people teaching false doctrine that departs from the truth of scripture. The apostle Paul, in his letter to Timothy, refers to a false teacher for the third time:

> If anyone teaches a different doctrine and does not agree with the sound words of our Lord Jesus Christ and the teaching that accords with godliness, he is puffed up with conceit and understands nothing. He has an unhealthy craving for controversy and for quarrels about words, which produce envy, dissension, slander, evil suspicions, and constant friction among people who are depraved in mind and deprived of the truth, imagining that godliness is a means of gain.
> —1 Tim. 6:3–5

Let's not commit the sin of craving controversy but rather have conviction about what we believe, preferring quiet confidence to quarrels and firm faith to friction.

A House Divided Can't Stand

In the Gospel of Mark, we read of Jesus dealing graciously with the religious leaders despite their failure to recognize that the son of God was among them. They even accused Jesus of aligning himself with the devil.

> And he called them to him and said to them in parables, "How can Satan cast out Satan? If a kingdom is divided against itself, that kingdom cannot stand. And if a house is divided against itself, that house will not be able to stand. And if Satan has risen up against himself and is divided, he cannot stand, but is coming to an end.
>
> —Mark 3:23–26

Jesus counters that if he's working against Satan, then how could he also be empowered by Satan? After all, he's been healing people and casting out demons, which is not the work of Satan. Rather, his miracles were evidence of his identity as God's son. Either we accept his deity as the one true God or we reject him as lord and savior. A house divided can't and will not stand. Practically speaking, this teaching means we can't serve God on Sunday and then live like the devil the rest of the week and call ourselves followers of Jesus.

We also see the principle of how a house divided can't stand in the political realm. On June 16, 1858, Abraham Lincoln, upon accepting the Illinois Republican party's nomination as their senator, gave one of his best-known speeches:

> A house divided against itself cannot stand. I believe this government cannot endure, permanently half slave and half free. I do not expect the Union to be dissolved—I do not expect the house to fall—but I do expect it will cease to be divided. It will become all one thing or all the other. Either the opponents of slavery will arrest the further spread of it, and place it where the public mind shall rest in the belief that it is in the course of ultimate extinction; or its advocates will push it forward till it shall become alike lawful in all the States, old as well as new—North as well as South.[3]

Slavery was a growing problem in this country, and Lincoln understood the dire consequences of continuing down that road. The basic concept of slavery in the Old Testament means a loss of freedom or being held in bondage. In the New Testament, it also carried the meaning of spiritual subjection to sin or Satan (Heb. 2:14–15; 2 Pet. 2:19) but also had a positive meaning to signify servanthood to God.

Paul had experienced this kind of servanthood to Jesus and wrote, "Therefore do not be ashamed of the testimony about our Lord, nor of me his prisoner, but share in suffering for the gospel by the power of God" (2 Tim. 1:8). Share in suffering? How many of us would jump at the opportunity to take on someone else's burdens? Maybe someone you know is faced with medical expenses they're unable to pay for, and in good faith they come to you asking for help. Do you share their burden? Maybe there's work to do around your local church. Do you volunteer? The desire to share in suffering for the gospel as servants of Christ and members of our church communities should characterize the life of every follower of Jesus.

The Unification Process

In our quest to become more like Christ, we must draw closer to him. But when we seek him with all our heart, we should know that God will likely challenge some of our attitudes and ways of living. Just like the man on the subway whom nobody wanted to get too close to, we may discover that some people want nothing to do with us. Skeptics and opponents of Christianity reject the idea of Christ as the one true means of salvation. For them, the teachings of Christ are too narrow. And behind their rejection is often a desire to remain in control rather than submit to God and what the Bible says about truth and what's right. So, Christians need to be prepared to face opposition from many in our culture.

My youngest son, Ethan, used to cry so loud it made my teeth hurt. What did he want? I would go down the list of fatherly duties and responsibilities but couldn't think of anything I'd failed to do. It wasn't because he was hungry, needed a diaper change, or was sleepy; it was because he missed his mother. He was experiencing separation anxiety due to being apart from the one who had carried him for nine months in the womb. The emotional and physical attachment he longed for is similar to our longing for God. We are meant to be closely connected to him. Although we don't always feel this connection, the apostle Paul wrote that "nothing can separate us from the love of God in Christ Jesus our Lord" (Rom. 8:39). If nothing can separate us from God, why do we tend to build up walls between us and our loving heavenly Father? Why not allow him into every area of our lives, including the financial, social, and emotional areas we tend to leave him out of?

The apostle Paul urged the church in Ephesus to be "eager to maintain the unity of the Spirit in the bond of peace" (Eph. 4:3). If we are to tear down the walls that divide us internally from others and from God, we must experience the peace of Christ in our hearts. Turmoil inside creates division on the outside. Thus, "Blessed are the peacemakers, for they shall be called sons of God" (Matt. 5:9). A peacemaker is someone who resolves conflict and facilitates reconciliation. There are many of us standing by, waiting for peace, when God requires us to actively engage in the peacemaking process. The scriptures say we're to "live peaceably with all" (Rom. 12:18) and even "strive for peace" (Heb. 12:14). Perhaps the book of James summarizes it best: "But the wisdom from above is first pure, then peaceable, gentle, open to reason, full of mercy and good fruits, impartial and sincere" (James 3:17). If we desire to live in harmony with our neighbors, then our objective should be to pursue peace with great diligence.

> Turmoil inside creates
> division on the outside.

In our society, peace can have a different meaning. To many people, peace might be found in the pursuit of money, becoming rich, and finding a sense of security in their possessions. But that can be a risky investment in the search for peace. Investors use a term *margin of safety*, which means that when market prices are significantly below the intrinsic value, an investment can be made with minimal risk. The truth is, however, that no matter how safe an investment may appear, there is always risk involved. No one knows what tomorrow will bring. Therefore, Jesus advised us to invest in the only sure investment—the kingdom of God.

Do not lay up for yourselves treasures on earth, where moth and rust destroy and where thieves break in and steal, but lay up for yourselves treasures in heaven, where neither moth nor rust destroys and where thieves do not break in and steal. For where your treasure is, there your heart will be also.
—Matt. 6:19–21

If you are a Christian, the Bible says you are united with Christ, and there is no wall that can divide that eternal union. Whatever walls you might have erected in your life that are keeping you away from the close, personal relationship God wants with you—whether money, relationships, addictions, or success—agree with your heavenly Father that nothing can separate you from his unwavering love. He will keep pursuing you and breaking down the walls that shouldn't be there. He is gloriously the same yesterday, today, and forever, and that blessed truth is all you need to remember while you live out the gospel message right where God has placed you.

Chapter 2

Inspecting the Walls of Our Soul

"I went out by night by the Valley Gate
to the Dragon Spring and to the Dung Gate,
and I inspected the walls of Jerusalem that
were broken down and its gates that
had been destroyed by fire."

—Neh. 2:13

In 2009, my wife and I decided to buy our first home. It was a long time coming since we had lived from apartment to apartment for the previous six years. To find a place we could call home was finally about to become a reality—that is, until suddenly the process was put on hold. We were told by our real estate agent that the home inspection had failed, and before we could move forward, we had to repair the basement walls, remedy a termite problem, and bring everything else up to code. The homeowner wouldn't pay to get it fixed, so we had to come up with the money to pay for the repairs on our own if we wanted to buy the house. Long story short, I ended up doing the repairs myself, and the second time around, the building inspector deemed the house acceptable.

Home inspections ensure that a house is in good condition before it can be sold. The inspector must be qualified and extremely meticulous when conducting the inspection. Nothing can be left to chance or presumed to be in good condition. If something is missing or needs upgrading, then it's the responsibility of the purchaser or buyer to fix the problem. Once all the repairs are made, the deal can be closed. Similarly, sometimes our spiritual lives need a thorough inspection and some repairs.

Cupbearer to the King

The book of Nehemiah is an account of God keeping his covenant with the people of Israel despite their lack of faith. God had promised them that if they continued to obey him, he would shower blessings on the entire nation. However, if they refused to faithfully serve him, judgment would come upon them, and he would allow them to be taken captive by their enemies. Sadly, they choose to rebel, falling into idolatry and engaging in immoral practices. True to God's promise of judgment, the Northern Kingdom of Israel fell to the Assyrians in 722 BC. Several centuries later, the Babylonians conquered the Southern Kingdom, and God's people were held in captivity for 70 years (Jer. 25:11). That's a steep price to pay for being disobedient. God was dealing with an immature and rebellious nation who had disregarded him completely, and they had to learn some tough lessons.

Despite this dark period, God uses a Jewish man named Nehemiah to bring glory back to the city of Jerusalem and the people of Israel. Nehemiah was a cupbearer for the Persian King Artaxerxes. It was Nehemiah's job to test the wine, assuring it was safe to drink, before offering it to the king. One day, while serving in this role, Nehemiah received a troubling report from men who had come from Judah.

> Now it happened in the month of Chislev, in the twentieth year, as I was in Susa the citadel, that Hanani, one of my brothers, came with certain men from Judah. And I asked them concerning the Jews who

escaped, who had survived the exile, and concerning Jerusalem. And they said to me, "The remnant there in the province who had survived the exile is in great trouble and shame. The wall of Jerusalem is broken down, and its gates are destroyed by fire."

—Neh. 1:1–3

Let Your Voice Be Heard

The report instantly depressed Nehemiah, and he entered into a time of continual prayer and fasting. He confessed the sins of Israel and reminded God of his covenant with Moses and his promise to restore the people of Israel if they returned to him. Nehemiah's prayer is instructive to us because when we are faced with horrible news, we tend to immediately ask for God's intervention without also confessing our sins and acknowledging any part we may have played in what is happening to us.

Notice also that Nehemiah prayed on behalf of the people of Israel. He wasn't just concerned about himself. He wasn't even in Jerusalem at the time, yet he cared about what was happening there. How we pray and what we pray for reveals what's important to us. Sometimes we say we'll pray for someone but then forget all about it. Nehemiah teaches us to pray with humility before God and with love for others.

> How we pray
> and what we pray for
> reveals what's important to us.

Prayer involves our whole person, and Nehemiah was praying with passionate resolve. E.M. Bounds, in his book *The Essentials of Prayer*, explains it this way:

> Prayer has to do with the entire man. Prayer takes in man in his whole being, mind, soul and body. It takes the whole man to pray and prayer affects the entire man in its gracious results. As the whole nature of man enters into prayer, so also all that belongs to man is the beneficiary of prayer.[1]

Nehemiah understood what it meant to be fully consecrated to God in prayer. In fact, his countenance had become sad because of what was happening in Jerusalem. That was unbecoming before the royal presence of the king, but he couldn't help himself.

Commissioned to Go

Among my favorite films of all time is *The Lord of the Rings* trilogy. If you haven't seen those three movies, I implore you to invest some time in watching them. Your life will never be the same.

The first movie in the trilogy, *The Fellowship of the Ring*, begins with a young Hobbit named Frodo Baggins whose purpose throughout the film is to destroy the ring that possesses the power to enslave the world. The quest begins when Frodo's uncle, Bilbo Baggins, finds a mystical ring in a cave. The ring becomes irresistible to the one who possesses it. After years of holding onto it, Bilbo decides it is time to pass it on to Frodo. After a long conversation with Gandalf the Grey about the history of the ring, Frodo is first inclined to hide the ring so no one will find it.

Before I continue discussing Frodo and the ring, I want to ask a quick question: How many of us, when called for a divine purpose, either make excuses or try to come up with another plan? Too often, fear diminishes our faith and weakens our resolve to fulfill the calling God has given us. That should not be. Following Christ requires courage. Now, back to Frodo.

The ring is no longer safe in the Shire, and imminent doom will soon befall the hobbits if the ring stays there much longer. Hearing this news, Frodo immediately reacts, as any of us would, and offers it to Gandalf to take with him out of the Shire. Feeling frightened and inadequate, Frodo wants to play it safe and let somebody else take care of the problem. Am I the only one who has ever felt this way when given a task to complete? I can remember many times in ministry when I was given an assignment and either declined or pretended like I knew what I was doing. Over the years, I've learned to say no to certain ministry opportunities and focus on the ones to which I've been called. That's not to say we shouldn't venture out and explore new ministry endeavors, but once we've been given the ring, so to speak, it's our mission to do something with it.

Frodo eventually steps up to the challenge and teams up with his friend Sam to destroy the ring. The following conversation occurs near the beginning of their journey:

Sam: This is it.
Frodo: This is what?

Sam: If I take one more step, it will be the farthest away from home I've ever been.

Frodo: Come on, Sam. Remember what Bilbo used to say. . .it's a dangerous business, Frodo, going out your door. . .you step onto the road, and if you don't keep your feet, there's no knowing where you might be swept off to.[2]

Like Frodo and Sam, Nehemiah had a mission before him that would require great courage. The king noticed something was wrong with Nehemiah and asked him what it was. Nehemiah made his request known to the king.

And I said to the king, "If it pleases the king, and if your servant has found favor in your sight, that you send me to Judah, to the city of my fathers' graves, that I may rebuild it."

—Neh. 2:5

This was a risky request to make to a king. It would mean Nehemiah would be away from his royal duties. Just as Frodo's faithful companion Sam had to take the next step out of his comfort zone and into a place of unfamiliarity, we won't know how far God will take us unless we kick our feet and move forward.

Soul Searching

As we labor in our everyday nine-to-five profession, pay the bills, mow the lawn, pick up the kids from school, and prepare dinner, have we forgotten to inspect the attitude of our souls? I can remember the exact time I first encountered the living God in my life. I was 16 years old and had already experienced family hardships, the loss of my mother, drug and alcohol addiction, gang activity—all things that were leading me down the wrong path. I found myself in a dark place, hidden from the world and engulfed in my own selfish ambitions. I thought the church was a bunch of religious zealots whose sole purpose was to detox the world with morality and their view of eternal salvation. During that time, I became bitter and angry at myself and especially at God.

To give you a little background, I was raised a Catholic and attended parochial school throughout my childhood. Long, tedious hours of catechism classes, serving as an altar boy, and making my way up the blessed sacrament chain did not produce a fulfilling relationship with God. It wasn't that the material had no effect on my life, but I tried to fill the empty void inside with the things of this world. Growing up in Brooklyn, New York, in what you could call the ghetto, I was not surrounded by exquisite things. Don't get me wrong, my parents tried their best to satisfy my cravings for the latest video games or action figures, but trying to keep up with the Joneses wasn't possible at that time. During my adolescent years, I continued to struggle with feelings that I didn't have what others had. At the same time, I was trying to become something I wasn't, forcing my character to mimic what everyone deemed acceptable. Soon, the effects of drugs and alcohol controlled my thoughts, and the god of this age had yet another deceived follower. At night, I would cry myself to sleep in hopes of being rescued from this hellacious nightmare that never seemed to have an ending. The broad path I was on led to dire consequences filled with false delusions of grandeur and the inevitable slow death of any remaining hope I had. How would I get out of this, and was I destined to live the rest of my days in turmoil and chaotic disorder?

One day, as I was walking down a dark, desolate road, the memories of failure and the feelings of being unloved consumed me. The thought of becoming a self-martyr, taking my own life, crept into my mind as the only way of escape from the pain that was lodged deep within my soul. As I continued to ponder this idea, I noticed a small bridge overlooking the highway. Making my way to the center of the bridge, I could see vehicles passing below, rushing to their destinations. I wondered if they noticed that I'd edged out beyond the protective railing and was standing within a few inches of harm's way. As I stood there, engaged in a fierce inner battle to find hope, grace made its way into the corners of my soul. I still refer to this as my Damascus road experience; it was at that moment that I understood what my purpose was. I began to descend from the bridge and immediately fell to my knees. My cry could be heard blocks away, but I didn't care. I understood at that moment that God loved me "before the foundation of the world" (John 17:24). That discovery and the rebirth of my faith remain with me decades later as I type these words.

So what was it that drove me to search for the meaning of my existence? Basically, I realized I was lost, but God could save me. Charles Spurgeon wrote:

> If you are not lost, what do you want with a Savior? Should the shepherd go after those who never went astray? Why should the woman sweep her house for the bits of money that were never out of her purse? No, the medicine is for the diseased; the quickening is for the dead; the pardon is for the guilty; liberation is for those who are bound: the opening of eyes is for those who are blind. How can the Savior, and His death upon the cross, and the gospel of pardon, be accounted for, unless it is upon the supposition that men are guilty and worthy of condemnation? The sinner is the gospel's reason for existence.[3]

I had finally discovered what my soul longed for—the forgiveness found at the cross, and my soul wanted to experience the salvation that comes by grace through faith. It wanted to know God. David's poetic line in Psalm 42:1 describes how I felt: "As a deer pants for flowing streams, so pants my soul for you, O God." I was desperately thirsty for the living God.

The Journey Ahead

Returning to Nehemiah's story, we read that the king granted Nehemiah's request to visit the walls of Jerusalem, and he was even given a military escort (Neh. 2:9). Upon arriving, however, Nehemiah was immediately faced with opposition. "It displeased them greatly that someone had come to seek the welfare of the people of Israel" (Neh. 2:10). Nehemiah would soon learn that his biggest problem was not the enemies surrounding the exterior of the city but the enemies within the city gates.

In our day, some of our biggest problems can actually arise from within the church. An internal struggle for dominance and control often causes division within the ranks of the local assembly. I have seen many churches split for various reasons, and it's usually the members who end up suffering the most.

Nehemiah was facing opposition from powerful men who were trying to stop his plan to rebuild the wall. Because of them, Nehemiah traveled by night (Neh. 2:12) to avoid detection by those seeking to harm him. That came with its own dangers. As a police officer, I can tell you that most crimes in America occur during the dark of night when criminals feel like they won't get caught.

Maybe the wall you're facing today seems enormous; maybe you're afraid you might fail to complete what God is calling you to do. The truth is, you won't know unless you try. It's that first step into the unknown that can set the course for completing your mission. Walk with confidence and not in your human ability or achievements. A Christian's confidence should be totally grounded in God's word, his promises, and his character. At the same time, you'll want to avoid overconfidence and continue to work hard.

I love watching the training scenes in the *Rocky* movies. There's just something about carrying a six-

A Christian's confidence should be totally grounded in God's word, his promises, and his character.

foot log through 10 inches of snow that makes me want to go out and conquer the world. When Rocky is preparing to face the Russian champion, he goes to a dilapidated cabin with poor lighting and no extravagant gym equipment. Makes you just want to sign up, right? In the meantime, his opponent, Ivan Drago, is training in an elaborate state-of-the-art facility with advanced equipment and a whole team of doctors monitoring his progress. The scene cuts back and forth between these two boxers—Rocky chopping wood and Ivan sending his sparring partners to the canvas. Rocky doubts he can win until his wife catches a flight to Russia to encourage him, causing his whole attitude and way of training to dramatically shift and intensify. He begins to train in the dark and adapt to the harsh elements of the country. Rocky ends up winning the fight and redeeming the painful loss of his friend who was killed by the Russian.

Never Eat Alone

What is stopping you from achieving the things God is calling you to do? Our journey of obedience is made much more difficult when we try to go at it alone. Nehemiah had some help. He traveled with a few men to inspect the walls of Jerusalem (Neh. 2:12). Many of us are afraid to ask for help. I'm guilty of this sometimes, and my reasoning is mainly that I don't want to inconvenience anyone. But I need help, and God calls us to help each other. The calling of the 12 disciples is an example of the type of bond and camaraderie we should experience together.

According to Mark's Gospel, Jesus called the first disciples, Simon and Andrew, who were fishing alongside the Sea of Galilee. "Jesus said to them, 'Follow me, and I will make you become fishers of men.' And immediately they left their nets and followed him" (Mark 1:17–18). One key ingredient we miss when reading this is that you can't have a relationship with Christ unless he calls you. These men had the opportunity to disregard the beckoning call of the Messiah. I probably would have said something along these lines: *And who in the world are you, and why should I even listen?* Maybe it's the New Yorker in me that tends to create a hard shell on the outside, distancing myself from anything that will cause an interruption of my plan. It's hard to let go of the things that give us a sense of identity and security, things such as careers and possessions.

Nevertheless, the disciples dropped everything and followed Jesus.

God calls us to work alongside others, sharing a common purpose. Building lifelong partnerships that change us and challenge our character is key to any successful ministry or venture. But what is really keeping us from developing these kinds of relationships with others?

Jesus surrounded himself with 12 unlikely men, each with different gifts but complementing the whole. These men ate together, stayed in the same places together, experienced hardships together, and laughed and cried together. The relationships we build must be based on trust and a shared purpose, not superficial differences such as race, gender, or economic status. Creating an atmosphere that invites others to join us on a mission for God is exactly what Jesus demonstrated with his disciples. We should never take on a mission alone. We need each other.

Chapter 3

Restoring the Broken Pieces

"And I told them of the hand of my God that
had been upon me for good, and also of the words
that the king had spoken to me. And they said,
'Let us rise up and build.' So they strengthened
their hands for the good work."

—Neh. 2:18

On September 11, 2001, a devastating terrorist
attack occurred on American soil, claiming the lives
of nearly 3,000 people and injuring more than 6,000
others. Two planes crashed into the north and south
towers of the World Trade Center in New York
City, and a once magnificent structure that stood
110 stories high collapsed to the ground, causing a
sea of debris that blanketed lower Manhattan. The

phrase Never Forget serves as a reminder of that terrible day and is still meaningful today.

A frequently asked question is where were you during the attacks on 9/11? Now if you asked me when the last time I heard a particular song or bought a CD (they still make those?), I couldn't tell you, but almost everyone can recall where he or she was during the events of 9/11. At the time, I was attending Bible college in Rhode Island where we had a chapel service every morning. On that day, I woke up like any other, brushed my teeth, got dressed, ate breakfast, and went to the service, carrying my oversized Bible in one hand and my textbooks in the other. After sitting down, the service started, and the worship leader asked us to stand for worship. We sang a few contemporary songs, and the atmosphere was charged with enthusiastic praise and a sweet sense of the presence of God. That would soon change, however, as I noticed a young woman running up to the stage with a look of concern on her face. She approached the speaker who had his sermon prepped and ready, whispering something I couldn't make out. The speaker soon began sobbing hysterically. After mustering enough strength, he told the faculty, staff, and students that there was an attack in New York City. At the time, there were only a few of us at the college who were from New York City, and when we heard the news, we all ran outside, frantic and concerned for our loved ones. I tried calling my family to see if they were okay, but due to the attacks, cell phone service was out almost everywhere. I fell to my knees, weeping uncontrollably, not knowing what the outcome would be.

Broken but Not Bound

The 9/11 attacks will always be remembered as a terrible tragedy, but that area of New York City has been rebuilt from the ashes. Nehemiah knew what it was like to witness devastation, but he also felt called to restore the once glorious walls of Jerusalem that provided protection and sanctuary for its inhabitants. The desolation he encountered included broken pieces of rubble everywhere, stones overturned, and a pervading sense of hopelessness. So how was he going to turn things around?

Many of us find ourselves in a similar predicament. We believe that our brokenness is beyond repair. A friend once told me that after a plate shatters on the ground and you try to repair it, you'll still be able to see lines where it was cracked. Sometimes, our lives feel that way. They have been shattered into pieces, and we have experienced such a deep fracture in our spirit that it seems utterly irreparable. I want to say, dear friends, that our brokenness is the beginning of our breakthrough. If we decide to wallow in our pain and give room to faithlessness, we have already been defeated. Consider the words from the prophet Isaiah:

> The Spirit of the Lord God is upon me,
> because the Lord has anointed me
> to bring good news to the poor;
> he has sent me to bind up the
> brokenhearted,
> to proclaim liberty to the captives,
> and the opening of the prison to those
> who are bound.
>
> —Isa. 61:1

Our brokenness is the beginning
of our breakthrough.

In my current profession, I've visited many homes on domestic violence calls. The parents are arguing, and they often lack sufficient resources to provide for their children. Some of the worst cases of brokenness occur in the Section 8 or rent-stabilized housing buildings. When I've visited these apartments, I've often found there is a sense of disenfranchisement and despair. Typically, the residents are living paycheck to paycheck, and many are on government assistance. That is the harsh reality of most urban communities in New York City. Hope can be hard to find. Storefront churches can be found on nearly every block, but most of the time, their doors are shut, protected by iron gates that keep out people searching for answers and healing. How can we bring restoration if our doors are shut to those who need it most?

We need to make a decision to want to rebuild and restore what is broken and fractured, and it begins by settling the matter in our hearts. A conscious decision to work toward change is the first step toward restoration. We have God's presence and his infallible word to empower us.

After the death of Moses, God commissioned Joshua and reminded him to meditate on the word of God day and night, being careful to do every-thing that was written in it (Josh. 1:8). Our success will be according to God's word, not on our own wisdom or power. If you want to help fix the bro-kenness you see, give the Lord your weaknesses, your faults, and your sins and become open to his will so his redemptive purposes will be accomplished through you. Stop drinking from the well of your own brokenness and immerse yourself in the pool of promises that never runs dry.

Vision-Impaired

"Let us rise up and build." (Neh. 2:18). Nehemiah's call rallied his fellow workers. They could sense the urgency in his voice, and they collectively declared it as one great choir filled with enthusiastic praise. Even the high priest Eliashib got to work and rose up with his fellow priests to reconstruct the gates (Neh. 3:1). It took a visionary to see past their cur-rent situation and into the supernatural future God had for them. Nehemiah had a contagious passion that drew others to his vision. Seeing beyond the norm and visualizing the future can sometimes be easier said than done. It's not just a physical act of seeing but rather a spiritual insight given by God.

Lack of vision will leave us stuck, afraid to move forward.

Consider another visionary who couldn't see with his physical eyes. Born in Georgia on September 23, 1930, Ray Charles, who would become the pioneer of soul music, gradually lost his sight, becoming blind by the age of seven. This impairment didn't stop the young man's dream of becoming a musician. Despite not growing up with a father and losing his mother when he was just 14, he learned from classical musicians such as J.S. Bach, Mozart, and Beethoven and played the piano for various bands, earning $4 per night. In 1952, Charles signed with Atlantic records and became an international phenomenon. He said, "I was born with music inside me. . . . Music was one of my parts. Like my ribs, my kidneys, my liver, my heart. Like my blood. It was a force already within me when I arrived on the scene. It was a necessity for me—like food or water."[1] Creating music was birthed inside him, and he cultivated that vision regardless of his personal struggles. He visualized what he could do through music despite not being able to see it with his eyes. He went on to receive countless awards and accolades, and his musical influence remains.

> Lack of vision will leave us stuck,
> afraid to move forward.

You don't need to see what's ahead of you to move forward. It's a labor of love, a quest to "press on toward the goal for the prize of the upward call of God in Christ Jesus" (Phil. 3:14). Whatever vision God has given you, let it become your mission, breath it in, never lose sight of it, and when opposition comes your way, remember who you are in Christ Jesus.

Organizing the Team

Every great organization knows that it takes a team to fulfill the dream. Aspiring to become a lone wolf in a field that requires multiple workers is detrimental to restoring the broken pieces in your life and in the world. Nehemiah knew that, so he took a roll call, so to speak, to count the builders who would restore Jerusalem's wall. Like any good team, the group included people with different skills and talents. There were goldsmiths and perfume makers (Nehemiah 3:8), important officials and rulers

(Neh. 3:9,12), and even the daughters of the ruler Shallum.

> **It takes a team
> to fulfill the dream.**

The priests led the way, setting the tone for the others. They could have allowed others to begin the work, but their integrity and commitment to the cause led them to take the initiative. They served as an example for all to see, getting their hands dirty while fulfilling their spiritual duties. Leaders set the pace, motivating others to follow them. In other words, a leader accepts responsibility. That's why the book of James says that not everyone should be a teacher—there's a greater responsibility and accountability that goes along with that role.

Maybe there's a decision you've been contemplating but are afraid of what saying yes might mean. Go beyond your fears, knowing that God is pleased when you rely on him and step out in faith to do what he is calling you to do.

As you take on a challenge, each member of your squad should be able to promote your ideas and come alongside you for the long haul. You will need a variety of people to help you. Nehemiah understood the need for a diversified group. A true visionary accepts his or her imperfections and areas of weakness and brings in others who can complement those areas. A prideful person who can't admit the need for help won't get very far. Being fiercely independent goes against the idea of a team and is usually evidence of insecurity, not strength.

One of the greatest basketball players of all time, Michael Jordan, fully understood the meaning of teamwork. "His royal airness," as he was dubbed, had everyone repeating the phrase, "I wanna be like Mike." It wasn't just his individual talent but his reliance on the strength of the team that led to so many victories. He recognized that "Talent wins games, but teamwork and intelligence win championships."[2] If Michael Jordan needed his teammates to succeed, we certainly do, too. Sharing the workload in the restoration process makes things so much easier.

Strategic Planning

Restoring the broken pieces of our lives requires strategic planning. We've got to prepare in advance for what God is calling us to accomplish. Before any work can be done, we need God's help figuring out what steps to take. God has a plan for building us back up. That's one of the great things about following the plans of God—no one can prevent us from following his plan of restoration if we are willing to trust him. Don't get me wrong, others will try their hardest to remind you of your past mistakes and failures. They'll try to convince you that hope of change is futile. Maybe there's a friend or family member who reminds you of who you used to be. But every follower of Jesus is under new management, and change is possible. Just as the Lord rebuked Job's friends for speaking lies, he can rebuke those who try to hold you back. I've lost many close associates who would slow me down from reaching my goals.

After my conversion experience, many of those friendships dwindled away. Some friends couldn't grasp the redemptive work of Christ and the sanctification process that was taking place in my life. I had begun to put away childish things and focus my attention on eternal matters. Many of those friends drifted out of my life and back into the world. Jesus talked about the cost of discipleship. Listen to his words in Luke 14:25–27:

> Now great crowds accompanied him, and he turned and said to them, "If anyone comes to me and does not hate his own father and mother and wife and children and brothers and sisters, yes, and even his own life, he cannot be my disciple. Whoever does not bear his own cross and come after me cannot be my disciple."

In his well-known book *The Cost of Discipleship*, Dietrich Bonhoeffer went into great lengths about the call of discipleship and our duty to a gospel community.

> The call of Jesus teaches us that our relation to the world has been built on an illusion. All the time we thought we had enjoyed a direct relation with men and things. This is what had hindered us from faith and obedience. Now we learn that in the most intimate relationships of life, in our kinship with father and mother, brothers

and sisters, in married love, and in our duty to the community, direct relationships are impossible. Since the coming of Christ, his followers have no more immediate realities of their own, not in their family relationships nor in the ties with their nation nor in the relationships formed in the process of living. Between father and son, husband and wife, the individual and the nation, stands Christ the Mediator, whether they are able to recognize him or not. We cannot establish direct contact outside ourselves except through him, through his word, and through our following of him. To think otherwise is to deceive ourselves.[3]

When we answer the call of discipleship, God will lead us. He will help us plan our course. If we fail to plan, we do a disservice to God, ourselves, our families, and those we lead. Deciding to plan does not reveal a lack of faith. It's actually the complete opposite, especially when our plans are submitted to the Lord every step of the way. Planning can help us get where we need to go and bear much fruit along the way.

Faith-Filled Focus

Once the plan has been approved and the troops are primed and ready to go, you must act. Without exercising faith, nothing happens. Faith is a Christian concept, of course, but in general, it simply means to trust someone or something enough to act on what you believe to be true about this someone or something. That means faith from a Christian perspective is a trust relationship with God in which we are fully persuaded of his love and faithfulness.

> Without exercising faith,
> nothing happens.

Because of our faith in God and what he says in his word, we trust him to do the impossible and obey what he commands. A faith-filled life is a life of deep conviction and commitment rather than double-mindedness and turning back. So let faith replace your fears, understanding that the righteous are called to live by faith (Heb. 10:38). Your faith will help you pay attention to the details of God's will, not wavering or cutting corners to impress others. The opinions of people will not reconstruct the walls torn by a lack of faith. Only God can do that. Your faith is a gift from him (Eph. 2:8). You can't reason your way into faith. Theologian Thomas Aquinas put it this way: "Free will is inadequate for the act of faith since the contents of faith are above reason. . .That a man should believe, therefore, cannot occur from himself unless God gives it."[4]

Setting our minds on things above (Col. 3:2) focuses our attention on the challenges ahead of us. Distractions are inevitable and come in many forms, so concentrating on what we're setting out to achieve is critical. We need to pray every step of the way, depending on God's help. There is great value in taking every thought captive to the obedience of Christ— it gives us confidence and courage. But there is a huge cost to letting bad thinking or runaway emotions distract us from the mission. We see an example of this in the story of Peter stepping out of the boat and walking on the water toward Jesus:

> Immediately he made the disciples get into
> the boat and go before him to the other side,
> while he dismissed the crowds. And after he
> had dismissed the crowds, he went up on the

mountain by himself to pray. When evening came, he was there alone, but the boat by this time was a long way from the land, beaten by the waves, for the wind was against them. And in the fourth watch of the night he came to them, walking on the sea. But when the disciples saw him walking on the sea, they were terrified, and said, "It is a ghost!" and they cried out in fear. But immediately Jesus spoke to them, saying, "Take heart; it is I. Do not be afraid." And Peter answered him, "Lord, if it is you, command me to come to you on the water." He said, "Come." So Peter got out of the boat and walked on the water and came to Jesus. But when he saw the wind, he was afraid, and beginning to sink he cried out, "Lord, save me." Jesus immediately reached out his hand and took hold of him, saying to him, "O you of little faith, why did you doubt?" And when they got into the boat, the wind ceased. And those in the boat worshiped him, saying, "Truly you are the Son of God."

—Matt. 14:22–33

This scene follows the story of the miraculous feeding of the five thousand and points to Peter's faith but also to his doubt. Why did Peter fail to walk on the water all the way out to Jesus? Jesus had suspended the natural laws of gravity, a divine supernatural act, yet Peter didn't trust him the whole way there. Peter shows that walking by faith is a moment-by-moment experience. He needed to fix his eyes on Jesus rather than on the wind and the waves. This fisherman who was used to being on the sea could not master it on his own.

> Walking by faith is
> a moment-by-moment experience.

Notice that Jesus didn't calm the sea until after he rescued Peter. The sea was rough when Peter decided to walk out to Jesus. The other disciples were overtaken with fear, but Peter was walking by faith. Faith gives us courage to do the impossible. Unfortunately, Peter, like us, was prone to look at his circumstances instead of at Jesus, and when he did, he sank. We shouldn't be too hard on Peter, though. At least he got out of the boat. The lesson for us is to continue walking by faith, focusing on Jesus as he helps us overcome our walls. So get out of the boat of fear, take aim at God's will, and believe Jesus is with you every step of the way.

Empowering Others

After a decade of planning and development, the magnificent 1,776-foot-tall One World Trade Center, which replaced the fallen World Trade Center, was completed and became one of the tallest buildings in the Western Hemisphere. It demonstrates to people around the world that challenges can be overcome and what was once broken can be made whole again. Each intricate element of the building's design took a team of skilled workers from all sorts of professions. They worked as one, capturing the vision of restoration and seeing past the sad history of the tragedy that had occurred there.

No matter how devastating your current situation seems, you've been given power from on high to overcome every challenge you face. God empowers each of us individually and collectively as the church body to function as one. Paul speaks of this oneness in 1 Corinthians 12, where he talks about the body of Christ (the church) functioning as an organism. Diversity and unity are important in the empowerment of each member of your team. God in his sovereignty has allocated and empowered each one of us with the same spirit (1 Cor. 12:11), and any gifts we've been given contribute to the whole body, the church.

> A team functions best
> when boundaries are respected
> and people are given the flexibility
> to operate in their spiritual gifting.

God empowers his people to be a blessing to the world. At times, we may stifle the Holy Spirit's empowering work by not involving others in the rebuilding process. A team functions best when boundaries are respected and people are given the flexibility to operate in their spiritual gifting. Trying to do things on our own will only leads to an unfulfilled life filled with disappointments and insecurities.

Nehemiah's team understood this. They saw beyond the impossible and envisioned the reconstruction of the walls, brick by brick, layer upon layer, each person with a specific assignment, everyone working together toward the same goal. Materials that were seen as damaged and worthless became the very same pieces they used to rebuild the walls of Jerusalem, turning what was broken into something beautiful. God still uses the broken things in our lives to refine, reshape, and refocus us into his living masterpieces, showing the world what a great and awesome God he is.

Chapter 4

Operation Rebuild

"So we built the wall.
And all the wall was joined together
to half its height, for the people had
a mind to work."

—Neh. 4:6

It's never easy rebuilding something that has been broken for a long time, especially when it involves relationships. Marriages that began with the promise of love end in divorce, or perhaps friendships birthed from commonality experience irreconcilable differences. There have been three times in my life when a once vibrant relationship ended in silence. These three people were spiritual leaders who gave me the opportunity to work alongside them in a ministerial capacity. Everything seemed to be going according to plan until the friendships gradually began to dissipate. Phone calls and home visits grew scarce, and there was a disconnect from the mission and vision of the church, leading to frustration and even anger. What was once a harmonious relationship built on trust and brotherhood fell apart. Years later, while praying, I concluded that reconciliation needed to take place. I began to contact each person, repenting of my past actions and asking for their forgiveness. Today, I'm in touch with only one of these individuals, and our new beginning is an example of how humility and forgiveness can help rebuild a relationship.

How we rebuild is vital for living out our Christ-centered lives. In this chapter, we will explore the basics of spiritual formation and how to apply some practices to our hearts. This list is not exhaustive, but I've chosen the disciplines I believe are pivotal for growing in godliness. Expecting transformation to occur apart from intelligent effort is unrealistic.

The Practice of Prayer

In Chapter 2, we looked at Nehemiah's prayer, but I want us to take a closer look now at how the spiritual discipline of prayer deepens our intimacy with God. The first step in building a prayer life is admitting we have no idea how to pray. God wants us to empty ourselves of all spiritual pride when we come to him in prayer. It's the Holy Spirit who teaches us to pray with words and groans that are too deep for our finite minds to comprehend (Rom. 8:26–27). God expects his children to pray. He knows we desperately need his help. He wants us to come to him like children, boldly and honestly telling him what's on our hearts and asking him for what we need. The good news is that even before we ask, he knows what we need (Matt. 6:8), and our asking is indicative of our faith and fellowship with him (Matt. 21:22).

> The first step
> in building a prayer life
> is admitting we have no idea
> how to pray.

There are many different ways of praying, including silent, centering, contemplative, reflective, supplication, and intercessory. The ultimate goal of prayer is to know God intimately and experience his grace in seeing him answer. God has chosen to operate his universe partly in response to prayer. Consider how Moses prayed for the Lord to turn his wrath away from the people of Israel (Exod. 32:11–12), and God did. And then there's the familiar promise of 2 Chronicles 7:14: "If my people who are called by my name humble themselves, and pray and seek my face and turn from their wicked ways, then I will hear from heaven and will forgive their sin and heal their land." Our prayers matter. They should be sincere (Heb. 10:22) and offered with godly fear in deep reverence for God. There are no rules in scripture regarding the manner or posture of our prayers. If kneeling, bowing, spreading your hands, or standing is your preferred posture, then go for it.

The best way to learn how to pray is simply to pray. It's as if we're learning a new language for the first time. We actually become more acquainted with the language the more we hear it and speak it. Reading a book (even this one) will not teach you to pray; it takes practice, asking according to God's promises and guided by his Holy Spirit (John 16:13). Don't be afraid to cry out to God, expressing your emotions freely.

Start with a few minutes and work your way up. Plan times of prayer and schedule them, but allow for more time if you need it. Find a quiet place that is distraction-free, away from all electronic devices. Your Facebook and Instagram notifications can wait. I would also suggest that you bring a journal with you and write down any thoughts, impressions, or responses that seem important. Maybe a certain word or phrase keeps coming to your mind but you're not sure why. At the appropriate time, God will reveal its meaning to you.

The Practice of Reading Scripture

One of the most important disciplines a Christian must undertake is the regular reading of scripture. The question we must ask ourselves is whether we reading only for information or also for transformation. We're not meant to approach the scriptures as if we're reading a textbook in which the words are cold and ineffective, leaving us unchanged. The Bible is more like a collection of love letters comprising a single beautiful story, pointing to Christ and God's amazing love for his people.

To help us go more deeply into the scriptures than a brief reading from a devotional book, I'd like to suggest an approach to reading the Bible called *Lectio Divina* (Latin for Divine Reading). It's an ancient, third-century Christian practice that helps us pray through the scriptures with attentiveness, focusing on a particular word or phrase that God might be directing us to pay special attention to. There are four steps in the practice: *lectio* (read), *meditatio* (meditate), *oratio* (pray), and *contemplatio* (contemplate). Start by reading the selected text slowly, digesting every word and then pausing for a few moments after reading. Allow the words to soak in, and then reread the text, looking for a word or phrase that strikes a chord with you. Next, respond to God in prayer about how the meaning of the text might apply to you. Finally, remain silent for a period of time, allowing the word to come to life within you.

But isn't hearing God's word crucial to understanding it? After all, Jesus said, "Blessed rather are those who hear the word of God and keep it!" (Luke 11:28). Hearing the Word of God in a sermon is great, but it's not a substitute for also reading it yourself.

Donald S. Whitney, author of *Spiritual Disciplines for the Christian Life*, expands on the importance of reading God's word through this illustration that challenges us to make reading the scriptures a top priority:

Evangelist Robert J. Sumner, in his book *The Wonder of the Word of God*, tells of a man in Kansas City who was severely injured in an explosion. His face was badly disfigured, and he lost his eyesight as well as both hands. He had just become a Christian when the accident happened, and one of the greatest disappointments was that he could no longer read the Bible. Then he heard about a lady in England who read braille with her lips. Hoping to do the same, he sent for some books of the Bible in braille. But he discovered that the nerve endings in his lips had been too badly damaged to distinguish the characters. One day, as he brought one of the braille pages to his lips, his tongue happened to touch a few of the raised characters and he can feel them. Like a flash he thought, "I can read the

Bible using my tongue." At the time Robert Sumner wrote his book, the man had read through the entire Bible four times.[1]

> Hearing the Word of God
> in a sermon is great,
> but it's not a substitute for
> also reading it yourself.

The Practice of Fasting

When it comes to fasting, there are misconceptions and fears that it can look overly spiritual, legalistic, or fanatical. Throughout scripture, there is a connection between prayer and fasting that intensifies the supplication before God. Nehemiah, upon hearing about the destruction of Jerusalem's walls, "continued fasting and praying before the God of heaven" (Neh. 1:4). Fasting is temporarily abstaining from certain foods (or all food) for a spiritual purpose. In the New Testament, Anna fasted night and day (Luke 2:37); elders were appointed to the church with prayer and fasting (Acts 14:23); and Saul and Barnabas were sent out under the covering of prayer and fasting (Acts 13:3). Fasting might weaken us physically, but it strengthens us spiritually, helping us love God above all else.

The expectation to fast shouldn't be ignored. Notice Jesus's words at the beginning of Matthew 6:16: "And when you fast." He assumed his disciples would fast. Fasting is putting an exclamation point to our prayers. It increases our dependence on God. We fast to seek guidance, express our grief, repent, overcome temptation or habitual sins, experience spiritual breakthrough, and honor God. There are multiple ways to fast. There are fasts in which you abstain from all foods but not water (Matt. 4:2), partial fasts in which you eat certain types of foods (Dan. 1:12), absolute fasts that avoid all food and water (Ezra 10:6), and a community or congregational fast that incorporates the entire church body (Joel 2:15–16). The length of your fast may vary. The Bible gives examples of fasting for part of a day or fasting for 1, 3, 7, 14, 21, or 40 days.

> Fasting is putting an exclamation point to our prayers.

To fast is to heighten our spiritual alertness to God's presence, shifting our focus from our physical appetite and digesting the spiritual meal set before us at God's banquet table. Through fasting, we develop a holy hunger that can't be satisfied by anything other than God because we have tasted that he is good. So allow the Holy Spirit to direct you to fast as an aid to prayer and to experience more of God's presence. Maybe a time of fasting is just what you need in order to see God do a great new work in your life.

The Practice of Solitude

As a husband and father of two boys, there are times when the desire for silence seems like an impossible wish. Even as I type these words, I can hear screaming and yelling over video games in the background. Despite the challenges of getting some peace and quiet, we desperately need renewing times of solitude and silence. Recently, I took a personal retreat to a secluded place away from the noise, the news, and social media. As I sat in silence, overlooking the water below and admiring God's creation, the gentle wind of God's spirit refreshed me. In solitude, we unplug and withdraw to hear from God. I left that place feeling as if I had met Christ for the first time.

The Bible refers to silence as reverence for God (Hab. 2:20). In silence, the soul experiences rest and renewal. The psalmist said, "For God alone my soul waits in silence; from him comes my salvation. He alone is my rock and my salvation, my fortress; I shall not be greatly shaken" (Ps. 62:1–2). The voice of God becomes clearer when we get away from all the noise. Elijah, while going to Mount Horeb, heard the gentle whisper of God's voice (1 Kings 19:11–13), and even Jesus practiced silence when he was led into the desert to be tempted (Matt. 4:1).

It's in solitude and silence that we allow God to help us and learn how to rest in God's sufficiency for our life and ministry. There was a time when I had deep ministry fatigue from wearing too many hats. I experienced an inner exhaustion that affected every area of my life. My joy had turned into sorrow. We can become so eager to accomplish mighty exploits for the kingdom that we forget that the Lord will fight for us, and we have only to be silent (Exod. 14:14). Silence helps us regain spiritual perspective and discern God's will for our lives.

Take time out of your day to practice silence and see how it can renew and rejuvenate your relationship with Christ. Just sit at his feet and let him do the talking. Start with a couple minutes and then work your way up to longer periods of time. Bring a journal and Bible with you and write down your experiences. One key is to find a special place where you can escape. It could be a park, your basement, or even a closet. Settle into a comfortable position. Breathe, and allow God's presence to quiet your heart. Try not to rush or create something out of nothing. Give God all your burdens. Be still and know that he is God (Ps. 46:10).

Silence helps us regain
spiritual perspective and discern
God's will for our lives.

The Practice of Stewardship

We have the spiritual responsibility, entrusted to us by God, to carefully use, control, and manage the gifts of time and finances he has given us. We are exhorted to use our time wisely because it passes by so quickly (Eph. 5:15–16). The truth is that our time here is short and eternity is long, so every day matters. I especially notice this with my kids. It seems like they grow up so fast. I need to value the time I have with them now because it won't last forever.

Each of us is accountable for how we use our time. We need to consider how we're spending our time and make sure the things we're doing are glorifying God. Remember that a day is like a thousand years to the Lord, and a thousand years is like a day (2 Pet. 3:8). He's never slow in keeping his promises. We must redeem the time with things that honor God so we won't become like the rich man who wasted his life and ended up in Hades (Luke 16:25).

Money can be a touchy subject, but it's a key part of good stewardship. We have an obligation to provide for our families, and not doing so is a denial of the faith (1 Tim. 5:8). Our generosity is an indicator of our spiritual maturity and an expression of the condition of our heart. God owns the cattle on a thousand hills, and everything under heaven belongs to him (Job 41:11). Our giving should be an act of worship and should be done with a cheerful heart, not reluctantly. Many of us have trust issues when it comes to our money, doubting that God will supply what we need when we need it.

> Our generosity is an indicator
> of our spiritual maturity
> and an expression of
> the condition of our heart.

Fear of not having enough can prevent us from growing in our faith through learning to trust God's provision. We ought to give out of love for God and not from legalistic duty. Grateful, faith-filled hearts give willingly and joyfully. The promise is clear in Luke 6:38 to "give, and it will be given to you. Good measure, pressed down, shaken together, running over, will be put into your lap. For with the measure you use it will be measured back to you." As they say, you can't outgive God. We never give in order to get; giving is its own reward. But we can know that God is faithful to provide for his children.

So let your giving be systematic and planned. Try to increase your giving over time, trusting the Lord with each new step of faith. This isn't prosperity theology where we give in order to get back even more. It's not our money to begin with, so we shouldn't worry too much about trying to keep it. Giving is one way we can demonstrate our love for God and our focus on the things above, not the things of this world.

The Practice of Evangelism

Evangelism has many definitions, but I found one from a 1918 committee of archbishops: "To evangelize is so to present Christ Jesus in the power of the Holy Spirit, that men shall come to put their trust in God through him, to accept him as their Savior, and serve him as their Lord in the fellowship of his His Church."[2]

After my conversion, I made it my chief concern to share the good news with anyone I came across. Armed with a small Gideon's Bible, I walked up and down the streets of New York by myself and boldly (and perhaps a little immaturely) declared the salvific message of the gospel to whomever would listen. When some people responded with confusion or anger, I realized that my passion wasn't enough. In the words of Charles H. Spurgeon, evangelism "is one beggar telling another beggar where to get bread."[3] Being motivated by love was the first fundamental step to effective evangelism, followed by learning how to better contextualize the gospel so others could understand the hope inside me.

Many churches today suffer from what I like to call evangelophobia, or the fear of being rejected by unbelievers and skeptics alike. The secular challenge to Christianity, including relativism and agnosticism, can make evangelism seem difficult. There's often a need for a skilled defense of the faith (1 Pet. 3:15). We are called to make disciples (Matt. 28:19–20), and that obviously includes sharing our faith. Evangelism is not about trying to fill the pews or cleverly winning arguments; it's about accurately communicating the content of the gospel to restore hope to the brokenhearted and faith to the faithless. In a multi-faith society, we're called to be ambassadors of Christ, telling a lost world about the salvation he freely offers to those who will trust him.

Are you willing to obey the call to share your faith and make every effort to use your spiritual gifts for the advancement of the gospel? Becoming part of a missional community should be our goal. In his book *Center Church*, Tim Keller explains that the goal of Christians is never simply to build our own tribe. Instead, we seek the peace and prosperity of the city or community in which we are placed through a gospel movement led by the Holy Spirit.

> Evangelism is not about trying to fill the pews or cleverly winning arguments; it's about accurately communicating the content of the gospel to restore hope to the brokenhearted and faith to the faithless.

Get involved in your church's outreach events and with other local ministries involved in your community. When we obey the call to evangelize, our faith comes alive like never before. We know that we have to trust God, or nothing will happen. I'll leave you with this stirring reminder from Romans 10:14 about the need for evangelism:

How then will they call on him in whom they have not believed? And how are they to believe in him of whom they have never heard? And how are they to hear without someone preaching?

Chapter 5

The Writing on the Wall

"Immediately the fingers of a human hand
appeared and wrote on the plaster of
the wall of the king's palace,
opposite the lampstand. And the king
saw the hand as it wrote."

—Dan. 5:5

The feast was ready, and all the A-list people were there. The guest of honor, Belshazzar, had arrived, and the best wine was being served in goblets taken from the temple of Jerusalem as spoils of war. Laughter filled the air as they praised the idols they had made with their own hands. Belshazzar was on top of the world, certain that he and his kingdom were nearly invincible. Suddenly, the celebration was interrupted in a most unusual way:

> Immediately the fingers of a human hand appeared and wrote on the plaster of the wall of the king's palace, opposite the lampstand. And the king saw the hand as it wrote. Then the king's color changed, and his thoughts alarmed him; his limbs gave way, and his knees knocked together. The king called loudly to bring in the enchanters, the Chaldeans, and the astrologers. The king declared to the wise men of Babylon, "Whoever reads this writing, and shows me its interpretation, shall be clothed with purple and have a chain of gold around his neck and shall be the third ruler in the kingdom." Then all the king's wise men came in, but they could not read the writing or make known to the king the interpretation. Then King Belshazzar was greatly alarmed, and his color changed, and his lords were perplexed.
>
> —Dan. 5:5–9

The terrified king immediately called for his magicians to try to interpret the meaning of the writing on the wall. He even offered a huge reward to anyone who could explain it, saying, "Whoever reads this writing, and shows me its interpretation, shall be clothed with purple and have a chain of gold around his neck and shall be the third ruler in the kingdom" (Dan. 5:7).

God could have conveyed his message to the king in any number of ways, including through a dream or an audible voice, but he decided to get the king's attention through this mysterious handwriting on the wall. The king had been refusing to acknowledge God and had been worshipping idols instead. Like his father before him, his failure to worship the true God would cost him greatly.

When the king saw that his magicians couldn't interpret the message, he was told that Daniel could.

> The queen, because of the words of the king and his lords, came into the banqueting hall, and the queen declared, "O king, live forever! Let not your thoughts alarm you or your color change. There is a man in your kingdom in whom is the spirit of the

holy gods. In the days of your father, light and understanding and wisdom like the wisdom of the gods were found in him, and King Nebuchadnezzar, your father—your father the king—made him chief of the magicians, enchanters, Chaldeans, and astrologers, because an excellent spirit, knowledge, and understanding to interpret dreams, explain riddles, and solve problems were found in this Daniel, whom the king named Belteshazzar. Now let Daniel be called, and he will show the interpretation."

—Dan. 5:10–12

The queen had entered the presence of the king, unbidden, knowing that a political emergency was occurring, and the king needed immediate help. To her credit, she said that Daniel possessed "the spirit of the holy gods" (Dan. 5:11) and could interpret dreams, explain riddles, and solve the most complex issues. So Daniel was summoned to help them.

Then Daniel was brought in before the king. The king answered and said to Daniel,

"You are that Daniel, one of the exiles of Judah, whom the king my father brought from Judah. I have heard of you that the spirit of the gods is in you, and that light and understanding and excellent wisdom are found in you.

—Dan. 5:13–14

Daniel knew what was at stake but was not the least bit intimidated by the king or the others who were there. In fact, he turned down the king's offers of rewards and position, saying that he would nevertheless interpret the message for the king. That was grace under pressure. When you fear God, you need not fear man.

In the following sections, we'll take a closer look at each word written on the wall and see how we can apply its message to our lives today. Here's what Daniel saw:

MENE, MENE, TEKEL, and PARSIN.

—Dan. 5:25

Number Your Days

> MENE, God has numbered the days of your
> kingdom and brought it to an end.
>
> —Dan. 5:26

Leonardo da Vinci was one of the great artists of the Renaissance era. A gifted painter, sculptor, architect, and inventor, he is famous for many paintings, including *The Last Supper*, a masterpiece that took him about three years to complete. Born out of wedlock and lacking a strong academic education, he learned to use his hands in skills and trades, and that experience would serve him well in his career as an artist. He studied human anatomy to help improve his work. His dying words are said to have been: "I have offended God and mankind because my work didn't reach the quality it should have."[1] Whether or not he actually said that doesn't matter as much as the heart of the message—our time is limited, so we ought to maximize our lives for God.

The king, Belshazzar, had been confronted with three words that were measures of weight. Mene means *mina* (50 shekels) and was written on the wall twice, stressing the impending demise of the Babylonian kingdom. The king's evil reign would soon be over, and what did he have to show for it? That raises these questions: How will we be remembered when we die? Will we have lived a God-glorifying life of service, or will we have pursued our own selfish ends?

In Psalm 90 verse 12, we are told to number our days so we can get a heart of wisdom. We must face the frailty of our human condition. We've all experienced the sting of death as we've had to mourn the loss of someone close to us. One of the most difficult times in my life was when I lost my mother when she was still quite young. She appeared healthy and full of life but died suddenly from a brain aneurism. No one could have seen it coming. I remember sobbing at her funeral and even questioning God. Her memory lives on in my heart. Life is brief and fragile. So as long as God gives us breath, we need to value our days and lives for God's glory, knowing he alone is eternal (Ps. 90:2).

That means we must pursue a life of wisdom. Wisdom is found in God's Word and is made meaningful and desirable to us by the Holy Spirit. The book of Proverbs is filled with wisdom, but we must approach it with humility and reverence for God if we're to become wise. Proverbs 9:10 says, "The fear of the LORD is the beginning of wisdom, and the knowledge of the Holy One is insight." Similarly, Ecclesiastes 12:13 says to "Fear God and keep his commandments, for this is the whole duty of man." When Jesus sent out his disciples, he instructed them to "be wise as serpents and innocent as doves" (Matt. 10:16). Living wisely is a must if we're to glorify God in this broken world. Thankfully, God's wisdom comes to us through his spirit (1 Cor. 2:6–7). We are not left to figure things out on our own.

> Wisdom is found in God's Word and is made meaningful and desirable to us by the Holy Spirit.

So let's ask God to help us make wise choices that honor him and bring about positive changes in our local communities and in the world. Let's build on Christ's example of sacrificial service. Let's redeem the time God has given us, believing that the best is yet to come.

Consider Your Weight

TEKEL, you have been weighed in the balances and found wanting.

—Dan. 5:27

Daniel continued with his interpretation of the writing on the wall, essentially saying that Belshazzar was morally deficient. When measured on the scales of God's righteous judgment, Belshazzar's life didn't amount to much.

How do we measure up to God's standard? If God were to measure you on a scale of one to 10, what number do you think you would get? Thankfully, God does not assign us righteousness numbers, but that doesn't mean we stop pursuing holiness. One of the greatest evangelists of our time, Billy Graham, once told a story about playing a round of golf with Jack Nicklaus, Gerald Ford, and an unnamed professional golfer. After the round of golf, the unnamed professional was asked how it was to play with the other men. He became very angry and said, "I don't need Billy Graham stuffing religion down my throat."[2] He left in a rage and headed toward the practice tee with his friend following behind. He took out his driver and began furiously smacking balls. After he had exerted all his energy, his friend said to him, "Was Billy a little rough on you out there?"[3] The pro became embarrassed and said, "No, he didn't even mention religion. I just had a bad round."[4] Graham didn't have to utter a single word for his faith to shine through and cause this man to feel guilty about his own lack of faith. Romans 12:3 says:

> For by the grace given to me I say to everyone among you not to think of himself more highly than he ought to think, but to think with sober judgment, each according to the measure of faith that God has assigned.

The measurement God uses to judge people is faith. "Without faith it is impossible to please him" (Heb. 11:6). Without faith, we are powerless to use our gifts for the kingdom. The disciples, despite spending so much time with Jesus, often faltered in their faith. When they couldn't heal a demon-possessed boy because of a lack of faith, Jesus intervened. They couldn't understand what they were doing wrong. Jesus had to teach them that they lacked faith in that instance. To have faith is to take God at his word and rely on his power. It's to trust God's character. Nothing is impossible when the ingredient of faith is stirred into the mix. Not having faith is like baking a cake without the sugar. Sure, you can produce a beautiful triple-layer cake, but when you take a bite, it will turn your face different colors like what happened to our good friend Belshazzar when he saw the writing on the wall.

Complacency is the enemy of doing God's will. We must be prepared to overcome obstacles if we're going to succeed in following Christ. Dr. Martin Luther King, Jr. once said that the ultimate measure of a man is not where he stands in moments of comfort and convenience, but where he stands at times of challenge and controversy.[5] We are called to take up our cross daily (Luke 9:23), not just to sit back and allow others to do it. There's no time for laziness, complaining, or shrinking back in fear. Less we forget what Christ said:

Not everyone who says to me, "Lord, Lord," will enter the kingdom of heaven, but the one who does the will of my Father who is in heaven. On that day many will say to me,

"Lord, Lord, did we not prophesy in your name, and cast out demons in your name, and do many mighty works in your name?" And then will I declare to them, "I never knew you; depart from me, you workers of lawlessness."

—Matt. 7:21–23

> Complacency is the enemy
> of doing God's will.

We're not on our own; we can trust Jesus to lead us. We're to appear different from the rest of the world so others may say, *Wow, look at what God can do!* How weighty is your life when measured by your faith? Do others see you trusting God in good times and bad? Belshazzar didn't measure up to the righteousness of God because being righteous is relational. Our spiritual adoption as sons and daughters of God connects us to him in a personal way. No one is righteous apart from Christ; it is a gift that is revealed from faith to faith (Rom. 1:17).

The Breakup

> PERES, your kingdom is divided and given
> to the Medes and Persians.
>
> —Dan. 5:28

The fate of Belshazzar was down to the last word as Daniel made known its prophetic meaning. *Peres* means half-shekel and is a play on words denoting division or breaking up. The once powerful and feared Babylonian kingdom would be divided between the Medes and the Persians. The entire nation would be broken into pieces, culminating with the king's death. The king's unfaithfulness had finally caught up with him. God had had enough. The relationship was over, so to speak.

In 1962, Neil Sedaka recorded a hit song called "Breaking Up Is Hard to Do." The lyrics for the song can sound a little like a relationship with God that is on the rocks.

> Don't take your love away from me
> Don't you leave my heart in misery
> If you go then I'll be blue
> 'Cause breaking up is hard to do.[6]

Some seasoned Christians lament the passing of the good old days and have let their relationship with Christ grow cold. Their once close relationship has become routine and passionless. Sin has slowly eroded the foundations of their faith. Their once vibrant prayer life and hunger for God's word has dwindled to next to nothing. They have been lured away by the things of the world. This is a dangerous place to be. Romans 1:26 talks about God giving people over to their sinful passions. Jesus said we have to make a choice about whom and what we're going to serve. "No one can serve two masters, for either he will hate the one and love the other, or he will be devoted to the one and despise the other. You cannot serve God and money" (Matt. 6:24).

We're to make Christ first in our lives (Matt. 10:37), which means letting go of any sinful habits that keep us from following him wholeheartedly. Hebrews 12:1–2 says we should "lay aside every weight, and sin which clings so closely, and let us run with endurance the race that is set before us, looking to Jesus." So if we've grown cold, how can we get back the zealousness we had at first? It starts with repentance. Listen to Jesus's counsel in Revelation 2:5: "Remember therefore from where you have fallen; repent, and do the works you did at first."

We have to get real with God and quit playing religious games. We can't fool God; he knows our hearts. He knows when we've drifted away from him. Some of us might be looking for happiness through success or possessions, but those things will fail us, and God knows that. He is jealous for our love. He wants us to know him. "And this is eternal life, that they know you, the only true God, and Jesus Christ whom you have sent" (John 17:3). So stop "breaking up" with him over and over again. He promised to never leave you or forsake you regardless of how many times you push him to the side. Return to "the love you had at first" (Rev. 2:4).

A Tragedy to Remember

Daniel had interpreted the writing on the wall and was given the rewards the king had promised. He was elevated to the third highest ranking position in the kingdom. But this honor would be short-lived because the king was killed later that night. The fall of the Babylonian empire and the beginning of the Medo-Persian reign had arrived. The message of the writing on the wall is that there's a severe cost to ignoring the true God and worshiping false gods. The king's sudden demise is a warning to all who deny Christ. On the other hand, the story also demonstrates Daniel's courage to speak the truth and his deep loyalty to God, no matter what the cost. The commitment to follow Christ will be costly for us, too. It is filled with ups and downs, joy and pain, victories and defeats. If we trust Christ, the writing on the wall for us will not speak of tragedy but of glory. For "if we endure, we will also reign with him" (2 Tim. 2:12).

Do you have a love song for God? A small species of parrot called the lovebird actually lives up to its name. These little birds have a mate for life, and if separated, they exhibit erratic behavior, even becoming depressed. When they've been away from each other for a period of time, upon reuniting they will feed each other, transferring food between their mouths. That's a pretty intimate relationship. Our relationship with Christ is also meant to be intimate. We feed on his word. We want to be near to him, so we engage in spiritual disciplines that will help us know him better.

If you've been drifting from your first love, seek God's forgiveness, forget about the past, and look forward to better days ahead with Jesus. Sadly, the world is full of walking Belshazzars living for the moment and pursing their selfish ambitions. That never ends well. But God has so much more for his people. The greatest love story ever told is this: "For God so loved the world, that he gave his only Son, that whoever believes in him should not perish but have eternal life" (John 3:16). When you put your faith in Christ, you became part of this great story.

Chapter 6

Breaching the Walls

"You have breached all his walls;
you have laid his strongholds in ruins."

—Ps. 89:40

The deadliest and most destructive hurricane of 2012 was Superstorm Sandy. The storm left dozens of people dead, thousands displaced, and millions without power. Sandy was a tropical storm that grew into a hurricane before turning toward the US coastline. She made her landfall on October 29, destroying more than 80 homes by fire in Queens alone, including my neighbor's house. I remember the day as if it were yesterday.

The mood was calm that night. It was business as usual in the Perez household—homework, then dinner, and then off to bed. All that would soon change. Certain parts of New York City were told to evacuate because of the potential flooding that might occur in high tide areas. My in-laws live in a remote area and sought refuge in my house to escape the dangers Sandy might present. As evening approached, the gusty winds and heavy rain beat against the side of my house as if someone were slamming a door. The tension in the air was thick, and all eyes were fixed on the news to hear the latest developments. Then from a distance, I heard a scream outside. I headed toward the front door, and what I saw next would forever change our lives. The streets were covered with water, and it was rushing toward my house. At that moment, helplessness, fear, and shock gripped my soul as I made my way to the basement to turn off the main power. Water was bursting through the windows like a scene from *Titanic*, and I quickly made my way back upstairs. I told everyone that we needed to leave because it wasn't safe for us to stay in the house.

We began to make our way outside. We had strapped our youngest son, who was just a few months old, into the infant seat, but our car was totally surrounded by water. We began to make our way down the street, but the water level was a little below my chest as I held my son above my head with all my strength, trying desperately to reach a safe location. Finally, we made it to the house of one of our relatives, trembling and not knowing what would become of our home. Eventually, I worked up enough nerve to return home that night to try to salvage whatever possessions I could. When I ventured back outside, the water was even higher than before. On my way to my house, I noticed that our neighbor's house was on fire. Before entering my house, I checked to see if our neighbor was home, but she wasn't and hadn't been there all day. Inspecting my home brought me to tears. My basement was inaccessible, and there was a foot of water on the first floor. I felt like I was truly reliving the story of Noah and the flood.

We were displaced for nearly six months while renovating our entire house. Finally, we were able to move back in. We had lost everything—clothes, furniture, food, and even my library. Precious memories had been washed away in a sea of destruction. As the years went by, the tragedy became more of story to tell than an ongoing loss. In the aftermath of the event, I learned that the dam on the river adjacent to our home had been breached by the waters during the hurricane. The force that broke through that dam was a once-in-a-lifetime event that no one expected and that no one was ready for. That's how life is sometimes.

The Charge

The baton had been passed; Moses, now advanced in years, was restricted from entering the Promised Land due to his disobedience. Joshua (son of Nun) would lead the people of God to occupy Canaan. He was charged to be strong and courageous, follow the law, and never turn from it (Josh. 1:7, 18). His mission was clear—cross the Jordan and possess the land. The land was promised, but the people still needed to possess it by faith. God's guidance and instruction had to be followed, each step in line with his divine plan. This plan would only happen because of the covenant promise God made to never leave him. It's like when Jesus commissioned the disciples to share the good news and said he would always be with them (Matt. 28:20). God's presence is with his people.

Joshua instructed the people to prepare for the journey ahead. He sent out two spies who traveled to Jericho and found lodging in the house of Rahab, the prostitute. She hid the spies on her roof and sent the king's men on a wild goose chase looking for them. In return, she requested that she and her family be spared from the destruction that would soon befall Jericho. The spies told Rahab to tie a crimson cord to her window, gather up her family, and prepare to wait.

Israel crossed over the Jordan River with the ark of the covenant leading the way (Numbers 10:33). Joshua told the people to consecrate themselves, and memorial stones were placed to commemorate the memory of their crossing. These stones, which represented the 12 tribes, were a reminder of the power and deliverance of God. The Canaanites, quivering in fear in their homes, spoke of God's people being on the move. The covenant relationship was reaffirmed between God and his people through the rite of circumcision, a sign of God's election of Abraham and his descendants. Joshua was then confronted by a figure with a drawn sword—a divine messenger, the commander of the Lord's army. Like the time when Moses stood on holy ground, Joshua humbled himself and took off his sandals. The campaign was underway.

And the Lord said to Joshua:

See, I have given Jericho into your hand, with its king and mighty men of valor. You shall march around the city, all the men of war going around the city once. Thus shall you do for six days.

—Josh. 6:2–3

The city gates were shut, but Joshua had been charged by the Lord Almighty to conquer this once formidable city with imposing walls that seemed impossible to scale. So how would he fulfill the Lord's command? The battle plan was unusual, to say the least. They were to quietly walk around the city. This military strategy didn't make much sense, but God had promised, "I have given Jericho into your hand" (Josh. 6:2).

To charge someone with a task is to give them a special duty to complete it. The question is, what has God charged you with? It may look strange, like when Noah was charged with building the ark and not one drop of water was in sight. "But God chose what is foolish in the world to shame the wise; God chose what is weak in the world to shame the strong" (1 Cor. 1:27). He chose you and me, the foolish and weakest of the bunch, to execute his battle plan, and it takes faith to step out when stepping out seems crazy. We will sometimes receive criticism for following God, as Joshua likely did. Moses, too, had to learn to deal with criticism. The people kept complaining, saying, "Is it because there are no graves in Egypt that you have taken us away to die in the wilderness? What have you done to us in bringing us out of Egypt? (Exod. 14:11). They looked at Egypt as a place of relative comfort and security compared to the wilderness. This return-to-Egypt kind of thinking can tempt believers when God has charged them to go where no man has gone before (*Star Trek* humor).

Joshua and the Israelites continued to march around the city for six more days. The enemy saw this and could have rained down arrows on them, but God protected his people, which increased their faith. They knew that victory was coming.

When people think your mission is absurd, don't become discouraged; instead, become a person of greater faith, undeterred by the fear of people and determined to go where God leads you. He can make possible what seems impossible.

The Cry

> So the people shouted, and the trumpets
> were blown. As soon as the people heard the
> sound of the trumpet, the people shouted
> a great shout, and the wall fell down flat.
>
> —Josh. 6:20

During the American Revolution, at the battles of Lexington and Concord, the first British soldiers fell to the American army and the saying "the shot heard 'round the world" was coined. Today, this term is used to refer to an unusual event or dramatic moment in sports. We see a similar scene at Jericho. Joshua and the people would execute the divine battle plan by walking around the city seven times and then blowing the trumpets and letting out a thunderous shout of faith. At the completion of all this, the walls of Jericho came crashing down.

Scripture often speaks of shouting in terms of reflecting the joy of the shouter and the greatness of our God. But there's a place for the battle cry, too. Sometimes a loud shout is used to rally the troops or even intimidate the enemy. In Joshua's case, it let the enemy know that the people of Israel weren't afraid of the enormous walls and superior firepower they were up against. Translating it to our context, it can mean you're not afraid to let your voice be heard for Christ despite the position, power, or popularity of those who oppose God's work in your life and your calling.

Making our voices heard, even shouting, is a part of life. We shout when our favorite sports teams are winning, and we shout when they lose. We shout in distress (Num. 16:34), and we shout for joy (Prov. 11:10). Our voices can be heard at particular times and places when it matters most to us, but are we vocal about the things of God? Or are we embarrassed, even denying our sonship as Peter did when he rejected Christ three times? Our cries of faith against the walls we face will determine whether they will fall or remain.

So, make your voice heard and render the enemy helpless when you shout with the voice of triumph. Cry out to the Lord, not just during times of trial or tribulation but also when you're full of joy. Shout to the mountains to be removed and by faith that it will be so (Matt. 21:21). Sometimes it takes an audible outcry of everything inside of us to bring the walls of life under submission to the lordship of Christ. The authority in our voices reverberates with the tone of our election as God's redeemed people. We have something to shout about. So let your shout ricochet from every corner of the earth that the battle belongs to the Lord (2 Chron. 20:15) and death has been swallowed up in a victory (1 Cor. 15:54). The walls of Jericho came down because of the obedience of faith, and the shout that was heard around the world will forever be a sign to our enemies that greater is he who is in us than he who is in the world (1 John 4:4). The trumpets are playing the victory song even now, so let your every breath praise the Lord (Ps. 150:6).

> Our cries of faith against the walls
> we face will determine
> if they will fall or remain.

The Capture

So the people shouted . . . and went up into the city, every man straight before him, and they captured the city. Then they devoted all in the city to destruction, both men and

women, young and old, oxen, sheep, and
donkeys, with the edge of the sword.
—Josh. 6:20–21

The walls of Jericho had been breached, and
with that came the spoils of war. Joshua gave
clear instructions on how the city should be captured. Everything was to be completely destroyed
as a warning to other nations that a great victory
has been won against the detestable ways of the
Canaanites (Deut. 20:16–18). No mercy was shown,
nothing left to chance, except the silver, gold, and
other metals that were added to the treasury of the
Lord.

We can learn from the capture of Jericho and
its annihilation that invisible armor is necessary for
our battle against an invisible enemy. This adversary,
the devil, the ruler of this world, seeks to deceive
us and destroy the work of God in our lives and in
the world. He also blinds unbelievers to the gospel
message (2 Cor. 4:4), keeping them in bondage to
fear and doubt. Just as with Adam and Eve in the
garden, Satan has been actively trying to deceive us
so we end up as casualties of war. We are called to
fight the good fight of faith (1 Tim. 6:12). This war

is not against "flesh and blood but against the rulers, against the authorities, against the cosmic powers over this present darkness, against the spiritual forces of evil in the heavenly places" (Eph. 6:12). Satan's strategy was to remove humans from the place of blessing (the garden of Eden) so a universal curse would follow them all their days. The plan didn't ultimately work, however, because of the work of Christ on the cross to redeem sinners from sin and death.

Invisible armor is necessary
for our battle against
an invisible enemy.

Satan can tempt God's people, but there are limits to his power. A great example of this is found in the book of Job. Satan could only go as far as God allowed him (Job 1:12; 2:6). Even though God's people are under attack, we have been given spiritual authority, and no weapon formed against us will prosper (Isa. 54:17). As members of God's family, we are watched over by our heavenly father. Although Satan is already a defeated foe (Heb. 2:14), when we continue to sin and disobey God, it hinders our efforts to serve God fully. Sin attempts to seduce us away from God's plan. We must stand in God's strength, because while Satan has a plan for us, God does, too. The fall of humankind didn't take God by surprise. He wasn't baffled by what happened but immediately had a word for the devil: "I will put enmity between you and the woman, and between your offspring and her offspring; he shall bruise your head, and you shall bruise his heel" (Gen. 3:15).

In the book of Ephesians, Paul instructed believers to put on the whole armor of God. A soldier doesn't engage in battle if he or she is not properly equipped to fight, becoming more vulnerable to attack. Paul instructs us to withstand the lies of Satan. Each piece of the armor is significant for defending ourselves against the attacks of the enemy. The goal of the devil is to separate us from the truth of God and the victory we have in Jesus. It's a victory that is assured by God for those who believe. So let's not lose heart. Those who overcome will eat from the tree of life (Rev. 2:7). By God's grace and with his help, take hold of your life and let the victory you have in Christ guide you to perfect peace.

The Consequence

Joshua laid an oath on them at that time, saying, "Cursed before the LORD be the man who rises up and rebuilds this city, Jericho. "At the cost of his firstborn shall he lay its foundation, and at the cost of his youngest son shall he set up its gates." So the LORD was with Joshua, and his fame was in all the land.

—Josh. 6:26–27

After the conquest of Jericho, Joshua said that whoever would try to rebuild the city would be cursed and childless. The attraction of sin, the appeal of wanting to mimic society carries with it a curse. God's people must not fall back into sin, although it's a constant temptation. The world lures us with its lies of pleasure and ease. But we're meant to grow up and see these lies for what they are— delusions based on empty promises. If we don't mature through receiving and believing God's word, we will continue to act like a child who never gets beyond baby food. Look at Hebrews 5:12–14:

> For though by this time you ought to be teachers, you need someone to teach you again the basic principles of the oracles of God. You need milk, not solid food, for everyone who lives on milk is unskilled in the word of righteousness, since he is a child. But solid food is for the mature, for those who have their powers of discernment trained by constant practice to distinguish good from evil.

The devoted things were considered anathema in Joshua's capture of Jericho. Anyone who didn't adhere to the ban was subject to the miseries and consequences that the curse implied. Sin is costly. Not following God's commands comes at a price. If we settle for living a mediocre Christian life based on partial obedience, we will not like the consequences. The Corinthians suffered from this infant syndrome, and Paul told them that he only gave them milk because they weren't ready for solid food (1 Cor. 3:2). If I gave my three-month-old child an eight-ounce steak for supper, he wouldn't be ready for it. But if my son were an adult and still eating only applesauce from a jar, then something would be wrong. Part of maturing in Christ means growing in our understanding of the consequences of disobedience.

A youth pastor from San Diego, California, was recently diagnosed with tongue and neck cancer that leaked a chemical into his brain, causing his body to shut down and lose nearly 60 pounds in just a few months. He underwent countless surgeries, multiple rounds of radiation treatments, and two months of chemotherapy. In the process of all these procedures, he lost nearly 60 percent of his tongue. The doctors said he might never sing or talk again. At home, contemplating all that had happened, his wife bought him a piano to help him escape the mental and physical torment he was suffering. As he sat there, his hands placed on the ivory keys, he began to compose a song that would not only encourage those around him but millions of others around the globe. The decision to overcome this wall was made possible by exercising the gift of faith and trusting in Christ alone.

> Part of maturing in Christ means
> growing in our understanding of the
> consequences of disobedience.

We must exercise our faith, too. The charge is clear, the cry of victory is earth-shattering, the capture of our enemies is assured, and the consequences of disobedience are confirmed. Best of all, we can be confident that God will strengthen us for every battle we face. "But they who wait for the Lord shall renew their strength; they shall mount up with wings like eagles; they shall run and not be weary; they shall walk and not faint" (Isa. 40:31).

These Walls

You are greater
Than these walls I'm circling
You are stronger
than this army that I see
You are bigger
Than these mountains that I face
And I will choose to only praise You

This is my song, this is my dare
To worship You even as these walls are
    standing there
This is my song, this is my prayer
I will declare

Nothing is too hard for You
There's nothing You can't do
I'll keep my eyes my eyes on you, I'll keep
    my eyes on You
Nothing is too hard for You
There's nothing You can't do
I'll keep my eyes my eyes on you
And watch these walls start crumbling.

Even in the suffering I'll sing
Even in my questioning believe
You are always good, You're good to me
    and I will sing[1]

—Jason David Sluyter, "These Walls"

Chapter 7

Dedication of the Wall

"And at the dedication of the wall of Jerusalem
they sought the Levites in all their places,
to bring them to Jerusalem to celebrate
the dedication with gladness, with thanksgivings
and with singing, with cymbals, harps, and lyres."
—Neh. 12:27

In 2014, I competed in the mentally exhausting and physically demanding obstacle course known as the Spartan Race. The course consisted of 10 miles of 30 obstacles and resulted in many bumps and bruises and a few battle scars as a consolation take-home prize. You need to prepare for a race like this. Leading up to it, I decided to increase my cardio and focus more on calisthenics and interval training. On the day of the event, I felt like my heart was in my throat in anticipation of the start. With war paint on, I waited with the other participants until the announcer bellowed, "Spartans, prepare for glory!" Every muscle was ready for the challenge before me, although fear was mixed in despite the fact that I had prepared for an entire year, and I was determined not to be defeated.

As I made my way through the beginning of the course, I felt exhilaration and a sense of accomplishment, but it was a premature victory. One of the obstacles ahead was a 100-yard bear crawl through barbed wire, mud, and rocks. The slightest wrong movement could result in getting snagged by the wires. After what seemed like an eternity, I finally made it through the trenches and proceeded to the next obstacle. In front of me was what looked like a moat and a 30-foot wall. In order to scale the wall, I had to jump into the murky water, pull myself up to the top, and climb over the wall. All I saw were bodies dropping from the top of the wall, still exhausted from the previous obstacle. The wall was slippery, and all we had was a rope to help us climb over. After a few failed attempts, I conquered the obstacle and the course and vowed never to sign up for that race again.

Upon completion of the rebuilding of the walls in Jerusalem, it was time to celebrate with a joyous dedication to honor God that included singers and an orchestra. It wasn't just a celebration of the physical wall; it was also a consecration of the city and the inhabitants who had returned to a right relationship with the Lord. They set themselves apart for a sacred calling. This separation unto the Lord is also seen in the New Testament through the whole church (Eph. 5:26) offering a spiritual sacrifice acceptable to God through Jesus Christ (1 Pet. 2:5). The walls we have rebuilt must continue to honor the person of Jesus Christ in every facet of our lives. The following section will outline a few areas where we can wholeheartedly dedicate our lives to his service. As the apostle Paul wrote, "Now may the God of peace himself sanctify you completely, and may your whole spirit and soul and body be kept blameless at the coming of our Lord Jesus Christ" (1 Thess. 5:23).

A Beautiful Body

> I appeal to you therefore, brothers, by the mercies of God, to present your bodies as a living sacrifice, holy and acceptable to God, which is your spiritual worship. Do not be conformed to this world, but be transformed by the renewal of your mind, that by testing you may discern what is the will of God, what is good and acceptable and perfect.
>
> —Rom. 12:1–2

All around the world, the human body has been admired for its beauty. Society has idealized the glitz and glamour of Hollywood celebrities, mimicking the appearances of the stars in hopes of shining just as brightly. A false sense of value has spread throughout our culture and is making its way into the eyes and ears of our children. Is that what God intended for us? This conformity to the values of the world has detrimental effects on the way we view others, placing impossible standards of beauty on people rather than considering how God views people made in his image. Our culture pressures us to embrace this way of thinking. But our spiritual act of worship adheres to a different navigational system where the Holy Spirit leads us into all truth. Paul's exhortation for us to offer our bodies as living sacrifices was understood in the context of the Jewish sacrificial system where animals were sacrificed in worship. Because of Christ's sacrifice, there are no longer animal sacrifices to atone for sin, but we now offer ourselves to God, desiring to do his will. Our old life of sin is gone, and we follow the new and powerful way of the Holy Spirit, who always points us to Christ. Not only that, but God through his spirit provides a way of escape from temptation (1 Cor. 10:13). So we have no excuse for thinking and living like the world.

Recently, pride in the form of too much of a focus on outward appearance crept into my life. I began to exercise more often and developed a passion for weight training. As time went on, that caused a break in my relationship with God. The idea of building and shaping my body to make it look like I wanted captured my heart, and soon I would be consumed by it. My walls (in terms of healthy boundaries) were coming down, my defenses had fallen asleep, and soon I found myself in a place far from godly influences, friends, and spiritual disciplines. All my resources and energy went into this activity, and I even began to compete on a semi-professional level. In the end, I realized my relationships had been damaged and I was more broken, outward-focused, and self-centered than before. The desire to be admired by others rather than using my body to glorify God proved to be my downfall and served as a warning to others to keep all things in balance, even good things like exercising.

Maintaining biblical priorities and a godly balance is necessary to take good care of your body while also maintaining a healthy relationship with your savior. When Elijah was fleeing from Jezebel and faced with threats, he became weak to the point of wishing for death. God used an angel to minister to his physical needs. Jesus was concerned with the physical state of everyone he came in contact with during his public ministry. He healed and restored the bodies of the sick (Mark 5:29). In other words, our physical health does matter to God. But as much as we appreciate and in some ways even idolize the human body, God's design is for us to use our bodies in his service. That's why the apostle Paul subdued his body in the service of the Lord (1 Cor. 9:27). We've been given these bodies as a gift, and the grace of God renews us both spiritually and physically. In her book *Sacred Rhythms*, Ruth Barton talks about the danger of losing perspective in this area. "I, for one, did not want to fall into the excesses of a secular culture that placed inordinate value on physical features rather than the beauty and dignity of the human soul as it reaches toward God."[1]

> Maintaining biblical priorities and a godly balance is necessary to take good care of your body while also maintaining a healthy relationship with your savior.

So what does a dedicated body look like? In 1 Corinthians 9:25–27, the apostle Paul talked about how he disciplined his body:

Every athlete exercises self-control in all things. They do it to receive a perishable wreath, but we an imperishable. So I do not run aimlessly; I do not box as one beating the air. But I discipline my body and keep it under control, lest after preaching to others I myself should be disqualified.

Our mortal bodies are to be submitted to God because they were bought with a price (1 Cor. 6:20). It's not just eating well, getting regular exercise, drinking more water, and getting enough sleep that matters, but also dedicating them to the Lord. During the last supper, Jesus referred to the bread as his body and the cup as his blood. He was offering himself for us. The sacrificial significance in the death of Christ directs our approach to honoring the body as a living sacrifice. There is a sacramental way of using our bodies to obey Christ. As we get older, our bodies decay, and what was once considered beautiful according to culture will be seen as something much less than that. We view aging as something to be avoided at all costs. But as Christians, we are not so concerned with those who can kill the body but rather the soul of man. A glorified body awaits the followers of Christ. Our perishable bodies will experience death, but our eternal souls will experience an imperishable life in Christ and new bodies in the future.

A Mind That Matters

Have this mind among yourselves, which is
yours in Christ Jesus.

—Phil. 2:5

French philosopher René Descartes famously
said, "I think; therefore I am."[2] The ability to doubt
one's own existence actually proved it. But that kind
of thinking—and proof—differs greatly from having
the mind of Christ. Every believer has been given the
mind of Christ through the Holy Spirit. We are not
left to depend on our own thinking. Paul instructed
the Philippians to have the mind of Christ, which
in context meant to embrace a life of humble service
just as Christ did. In other words, having the mind of
Christ relates to how you live out your faith and rep-
resent Christ. It means to let your life demonstrate
love for Christ and others. It means loving people
not because we are commanded to but because we
want to, to love them even when they don't recipro-
cate, to love them when it's difficult to do so. That
kind of love is unconditional, just as God's is for us.
After all, while we were sinners, Christ loved us so
much he was willing to die for us (Rom. 5:8).

Unfortunately, we sometimes fail to love because of our remaining sin and selfishness. Our egos get in the way of loving God and others as we foolishly imagine that we have all the answers and others should serve us. Have you ever met someone who is never wrong? That kind of pride destroys relationships. Humility means putting aside your interests and thinking about what your neighbor needs. This is not a false humility that seeks to draw attention to ourselves rather than to Christ. That's what Paul was trying to say when he told the Philippians to esteem one another (Phil. 2:3). A selfish person is constantly looking for ways to satisfy his or her own flesh. The flesh has little regard for others. That's why we are told to crucify it, flee from it, and never indulge it. There's nothing good about the flesh.

> Humility means putting aside
> your interests and thinking
> about what your neighbor needs.

Renewal of the mind involves allowing God's word to reshape our thinking. In a world filled with lies and deceptions, that can be easier said than done.

So many men in our culture have bought into lies and are addicted to pornography. This temporary satisfaction dishonors the image of God in women and ruins many relationships and marriages. The normalization of this sin is exactly what the enemy wants. When we engage in such conduct, there is a potential for the images to replay in our minds, enslaving us even more (Rom. 6:16). But we are told in scripture not to allow sin to reign in our mortal bodies, making us obey its passions (Rom 6:12). If we do, our hearts will harden and grow less and less sensitive to the Holy Spirit's convicting grace.

The mind controlled by the Holy Spirit leads to a mind that focuses on the things of God. Our thinking and perceptions must be wired for godly intimacy rather than sinful substitutes. Many of us have wasted enough time focusing on worthless things instead of righteous living.

So what takes up most of your thinking? Are you more concerned with watching the latest sporting event or buying another pair of shoes at the mall than you are with growing your relationship with God? There's nothing wrong with these things, but they should not outweigh your personal relationship with the living God. Our attitude toward Christ is what's most important and should guide our every decision. We must know who we are in Christ—greatly beloved sons and daughters of the king—and as we meditate on this daily, we are conformed more and more into the likeness of our savior. So dedicate your mind to thinking often of the beauty and splendor of his matchless grace and give the glory due his name with all your heart, soul, mind, and strength.

Obligation of the Covenant

Join with their brothers, their nobles, and enter into a curse and an oath to walk in God's Law that was given by Moses the servant of God, and to observe and do all the commandments of the LORD our Lord and his rules and his statutes.

—Neh. 10:29

After the completion of the wall, Nehemiah made a firm covenant agreement of obedience and vowed to commit not only himself but the entire nation to the service of the Lord. This faithful response was a seal between them and their God that couldn't be broken. The stipulations of the agreement were clear, and the terms were laid out. They took this pledge seriously and vowed never to neglect the law as their forefathers had done. This solemn vow meant a treaty would be formed that couldn't be breached. It was meant to last a lifetime.

The Bible is full of oaths and promises that were made between God and his people. Christ taught that the meaning of an oath was binding. "Again you have heard that it was said to those of old, 'You shall not swear falsely, but shall perform to the Lord what you have sworn" (Matt. 5:33). An oath means you will fulfill your end of the agreement. But have you ever made a promise you couldn't keep? There was a time when my youngest son was begging me for a certain toy that had just come out. I assured him that I would get him the toy later in the day. As the hours flew by, I became overwhelmed at work and totally forgot to get him the toy I had promised. I didn't even realize it until I picked him up from school, and the first words out of his mouth were, "Did you get me the toy, Daddy?" At that moment, I felt like the worst father in the world, and the look of disappointment on his face would replay over and over again in my mind. When I broke the news to him, I could hear whimpering in the backseat. Needless to say, I vowed to never make that mistake again.

When we decide to follow Christ, it is meant to be for life; it is meant to be a firm commitment. We have entered into a covenant with God based on his faithfulness and his ability to help us remain faithful. That kind of commitment to faithfulness should also be reflected in all our relationships. Jesus exhorted his followers to let their yes be yes and their no be no. Saying yes just to please another person is to falsely present them with a promise that you might not be able to keep. So integrity and sincerity in our speech and in the promises we make to one another are of great importance to God. Our relationships should be defined by trust and mutual obligation, grounded in the unchanging love and faithfulness of Christ.

Many of us have been disappointed or hurt by others who have not remained faithful to us in some way. A relationship that was built with strong walls of love, faith, and devotion can come tumbling down quickly when promises are broken and trust is diminished. So we always need to make sure we're keeping our end of the bargain. The only way we will do that is if we rely on Christ, knowing that he is always faithful to us. And when others let us down, which will sometimes happen in this broken world, we need to forgive them as Christ has forgiven us. Then, we need to seek to rebuild what's been destroyed, trusting God to lead us and help us each step of the way.

Our relationships should be defined by
trust and mutual obligation,
grounded in the unchanging love
and faithfulness of Christ.

Chapter 8

A Word about Walls

"A man can no more diminish God's glory
by refusing to worship Him than a lunatic
can put out the sun by scribbling the word
'darkness' on the walls of his cell."
—C. S. Lewis

This book was written to help us recognize the walls that may be hindering our relationship with God and to help us rebuild and restore the broken pieces, renewing our purpose of living a God-centered life. Walls are inevitable, and they come in all different shapes and sizes. Some walls last for a short time and others for a lifetime. Walls are meant to fortify, protect, secure, defend, safeguard, preserve, and shield us from harm's way. But walls can cause division, anger, hostility, bitterness, immorality, and even spiritual death if they separate us from God. The manner in which we construct our walls is vital for healed relationships and joy in Christ. Our rebuilding project must begin with the chief cornerstone, Jesus, who is the foundation of a solid, sturdy, and satisfying life. The blueprint for such construction is laid out in his word. Every detail is available to us because he understands our weakness and came to rescue us from a futile life of pursuing temporary things that don't ultimately satisfy.

Writing this book has challenged me to go back to the drawing board and make certain that every piece fits the master's design; I know I can't build this alone. It takes a team of devoted followers to tell the world there is a road less traveled that is worth going down no matter what the cost. No matter how much you may feel like a prodigal, God pursues you and welcomes you back with open arms.

Walls have the tendency to distort our views of God, causing us to doubt his love and run away from him rather than run to him. But God has opened our spiritual eyes, providing a glorious, panoramic view of life through the gift of his son. God's grace in Christ fortifies the walls we need and tears down the ones we don't. Christ is our load-bearing wall that bears the weight (sin) of the world. Without him we become unstable and in danger of collapsing under the weight of our own sin and bad choices.

Whatever areas in our lives are causing cracks in our spiritual walls should be dealt with immediately. Leaving even part of them open to further damage will eventually lead to greater problems and more pain in our lives. We must rely on the carpenter from Nazareth to help us rebuild our walls to withstand the harsh elements of life's circumstances.

> God's grace in Christ
> fortifies the walls we need and
> tears down the ones we don't.

The walls we build also keep out the wolves that come in sheep's clothing. The nature of the wolf is to seek to devour the sheep. Figuratively speaking, the world seeks to devour us, too. But we are part of the great shepherd's fold, and when he sees the wolf coming, he is quick to act to protect and guide his sheep. In the beautiful imagery of Psalm 23, his rod and staff comfort us. No matter how dangerous our foes appear, the good shepherd leads us to victory. "You will not fear the terror of the night, nor the arrow that flies by day" (Ps. 91:5). Our spiritual walls of faith are designed to withstand every attack as we rely on Christ to strengthen us. We are not left on our own to fight the battles of life. Our foundation is none other than the invincible love of Christ (1 Cor. 3:11).

If we know God through Christ, we also know that God is love. His love for us is active and powerful and entirely based on grace. God pours out his unconditional love in us so we may enjoy him and demonstrate that type of love to others. Our friends and family should not look at us and see walls of hostility based on the past. Instead, they should see the new creation God has built and is continually building in us. This new creation is made by love and for love. We do not go on this journey alone. We need each other. Life, like the trinity, is relational at the core. You can't have a vibrant relationship with God and have all kinds of broken relationships. That's why it's important to have the right kind of walls in our lives.

Recently, I heard of a parable about three bricklayers. A traveler was walking one day and came across three men who were working at their jobs. He asked the first man what he was doing, and the man answered in a rough tone, "I'm laying bricks." When he asked the second man the same question he answered, "I'm building a wall." He then posed the question to the third man, and the man responded with enthusiasm, "I'm building a cathedral." All three bricklayers were accomplishing the same task, but only one man saw a God-inspired, bigger vision of the meaning of his work.

The calling we have is bigger than any one of us and bigger than our personal timetables. It will far exceed our expectations because God is involved with us, helping us fulfill our calling. That gives him great glory. The meaning of our lives is seeing God's big picture and joining with him to see it come to fruition. We find our joy in our relationship with him. It's what wakes us up in the morning, announcing, "This is the day that the LORD has made; let us rejoice and be glad in it" (Ps. 118:24). Increasing joy makes its way into the life of the faithful, even in times of trouble. Living with godly walls allows us to enjoy God and keep out the things that make us miserable. Every wall that is assembled with the help and guidance of the Holy Spirit points to Christ.

Test the structural integrity of your walls today. Does each area of your life demonstrate godly integrity? Or are there some areas that crumble under the pressure? Does the big bad wolf of adversity huff and puff and blow your spiritual house down, or does your house hold up under severe conditions? We've learned to recognize the walls that divide us and inspect, restore, and rebuild what was once broken. The walls of life will remain until the coming of the master builder when we will see a great high wall adorned with every kind of precious jewels. There, the gates will never close, and we will enjoy life forever as God's beloved people whose names are written in the Lamb's book of life (Rev. 21:12–27).

Soli Deo Gloria!

Notes

Chapter 1

1. Charles Spurgeon, *Spiritual Warfare in a Believer's Life,* ed. Robert Hall (Lynwood, WA: Emerald Books, 1993), 115.

2. Erwin W. Lutzer, *The Doctrines That Divide: A Fresh Look at the Historical Doctrines That Separate Christians* (Grand Rapids, MI: Kregel Publications, 1998), 32–33.

3. "House Divided Speech," Lincoln Home, National Park Service, https://www.nps.gov/liho/learn/historyculture/housedivided.htm.

Chapter 2

1. Edward M. Bounds, *The Essentials of Prayer* (Dallas, TX: Gideon House Books, 2016), Google Books.

2. *The Lord of the Rings*, IMSDB, http://www.imsdb.com/scripts/Lord-of-the-Rings-Fellowship-of-the-Ring,-The.html.

3. Charles H. Spurgeon, *Collected Works, Vol. 1*, Google Books, 90.

Chapter 3

1. Ray Charles and David Ritz, *Brother Ray: Ray Charles' Own Story* (Cambridge, MA: Da Capo Press, 1978), 8.

2. Michael Jordan, *BrainyQuote*, https://www.brainyquote.com/quotes/michael_jordan_167383.

3. Dietrich Bonhoeffer, *The Cost of Discipleship* (New York: Touchstone, 1959), 96–97.

4. "The Apologetics of Thomas Aquinas," *Apologetics Resource Center*, https://arcapologetics.org/objections/apologetics-thomas-aquinas/.

Chapter 4

1. Donald S. Whitney, *Spiritual Disciplines for the Christian Life* (Colorado Springs, CO: NavPress, 1991), 35.

2. *Commission on Evangelism* (Westminster, England: The Press and Publications Board of the Church Assembly, 1944), 1.

3. "Evangelism," http://www.biblecenter.com/bibleclasses/evangelism.htm.

Chapter 5

1. "Leonardo da Vinci Biography," *Biography Online*, https://www.biographyonline.net/scientists/leonardo_da _vinci.html.

2. R.C. Sproul, *The Holiness of God* (Wheaton, IL: Tyndale House Publishers, 1985), 67.

3. Ibid.

4. Ibid.

5. Martin Luther King, Jr., *Strength to Love* (Minneapolis, MN: Fortress Press, 2010), 26.

6. Howard Greenfield and Neil Sedaka, "Breaking Up Is Hard To Do," Screen Gems-EMI Music Inc. and Universal Music, Track 11 on *Overnight Success*.

Chapter 6

1. Jason David Sluyter, "These Walls," *These Walls. pages*, https://static1.squarespace.com/static/56cdfd9e 859fd0c6ab92819f/t/5969cb4e37c5813ffaf5a104/1500 105550761/These+Walls+-+Official+Chords+%26+Lyrics .pdf.

Chapter 7

1. Ruth Haley Barton, *Sacred Rhythms* (Downers Grove, IL: InterVarsity Press, 2006), 80.

2. "Cogito, ergo sum," *Encyclopaedia Britannica*, https://www.britannica.com/topic/cogito-ergo-sum.

About the Author

1. Charles Haddon Spurgeon, ed. Anthony Uyl, *Spurgeon's Sermons, Volume 11:1865* (Ontario: Devoted Publishing, 2017), 116.

About the Author

Born and raised in New York City, Edwin Perez is an author, speaker, and blogger who is passionate about people and seeing change in communities through the message of the gospel. Called to the ministry at the age of 16, his hunger for a deeper understanding of God's word led him to Northpoint Bible College. While he was there, he traveled throughout the New England and tri-state area speaking and ministering. After graduating, he returned to his hometown of Queens, New York, to preach the gospel to the unreached, focusing on outreach and youth ministries.

In his hometown, he worked for many years as a youth director and outreach pastor and wasn't satisfied until every encounter led souls to Christ.

One of his favorite quotes is by Baptist preacher Charles Haddon Spurgeon: "To be a soul winner is the happiest thing in this world and with every soul you bring to Jesus Christ, you seem to get a new Heaven here upon earth!"[1]

Edwin received his BS in Biblical and Theological Studies and is currently enrolled in a Master of Divinity program at Fuller Theological Seminary. He also loves coffee, working out, and is an avid collector of books.

He is married to Jocelyn, and they have two boys, Elijah and Ethan. Edwin regularly blogs at www.breachingthewalls.org.

Social Media Links

EdwinJPerez79

EdwinPerez

EdwinJPerez79

ejperez79